- highly engaged
- improving staff effec
- attrition

driven by leaders that communicate well
most important factor in program success

employees must <u>believe</u> leaders took
some action as a result of their feedback
< active / intentional listening

Leadership Effectiveness top driver for boost in
performance, engagement (well over pay, benefits,
incentives

The authors are highly successful pros in talent management strategies. Their new book brings valuable insight to the impact of leaders in every organization. It's a superb resource for anyone managing a team or leading an engagement initiative.

—Beverly Kaye
Founder, Career Systems International

Christopher and Craig have done a very thorough job of creating a guide on how to engage and to keep talent. There is nothing more important than the talent you bring into your organization, and retaining that talent. Follow *Talent Keepers* advice and you will move from good to great and great to greater.

—Lee Cockerell
Former Executive Vice President,
Walt Disney World® Resort and Best-Selling Author

Individual success and organizational performance—there are no more important topics in today's competitive world, and *Talent Keepers* shows how to increase both! Learn the strategies and tactics which will unleash the potential of your people to drive your organizational success. This book goes beyond data to understanding and action.

—Richard M. Vosburgh, PhD
Retired Senior Vice President and Chief HR Officer,
KEMET Electronics Corporation

talent
keepers

CHRISTOPHER MULLIGAN and CRAIG R. TAYLOR

talent
keepers

How Top Leaders Engage and Retain
Their Best Performers

WILEY

Library of Congress Cataloging-in-Publication Data

Names: Mulligan, Christopher, 1964- author. | Taylor, Craig R., 1951- author.
Title: Talent keepers : how top leaders engage and retain their best
  performers / Christopher Mulligan, Craig Taylor.
Description: First Edition. | Hoboken : Wiley, 2019. | Includes index. |
  Identifiers: LCCN 2018047798 (print) | LCCN 2018060301 (ebook) | ISBN
  9781119558279 (Adobe PDF) | ISBN 9781119558255 (ePub) | ISBN 9781119558248
  (hardback) | ISBN 9781119558279 (ePDF)
Subjects: LCSH: Employee retention–United States. | Incentive awards–United
  States. | Leadership–United States. | BISAC: BUSINESS & ECONOMICS /
  Leadership. | BUSINESS & ECONOMICS / General. | BUSINESS & ECONOMICS /
  Management.
Classification: LCC HF5549.5.R58 (ebook) | LCC HF5549.5.R58 M85 2019 (print)
  | DDC 658.3/14–dc23
LC record available at https://lccn.loc.gov/2018047798

Printed in the United States of America

V10008560_030519

CONTENTS

PREFACE

America's workplace has taken us on quite a run over the past two decades. Riding the dot-com boom that fueled the "war for talent" during the 1990s, the bubble suddenly burst in 2000, slipping us into a recession. By 2003, job growth, income, and employee optimism were soaring again, this time powered by subprime mortgages and suspect lending practices that, as you know, all came crashing down, starting at the end of 2007, sending the US economy into an extended funk. For too many Americans, employment opportunities dried up, wages stagnated, businesses closed, and growth largely came to a halt.

Thankfully, the long road to recovery began in 2014 and was paved with the longest stretch of continuous job growth in our history. In 2018, the American economy continued to grow and expand resulting in record low unemployment rates. The National Total Unemployment rate was 4.1%, a full point below the 5.1% rate which the US Federal Reserve considers "full employment." The unemployment rate for those with college degrees is almost half the total unemployment rate at 2.1%. For employees, if you want to work you have choices. For employers, if you want workers you have to be able to engage them in order to get them to stay!

Studying the American workforce throughout this roller coaster of a ride, we took a deep dive, looking for those things that keep people going at work in good times and bad. What we discovered motivated us to write this book, propelled by our desire to share what we learned.

What inspires people and fuels a commitment to their employers, their roles, and their leaders? How do "best-in-class" organizations retain great people while competition is fierce in areas like technology, healthcare, engineering, and even skilled trades? Are employers adapting quickly enough to keep millennials—the largest generation in the workforce—committed and inspired in their jobs? What impact do leaders, at all levels, have in building trust and strong relationships with their team members? Do leaders really understand the impact they have on their team members' engagement and decisions to stay or leave? This book explores these questions and many, many more, offering a series of practical strategies and tactics you can put to work within your organization and with your team.

We have the privilege of working with and learning from many of the world's most successful organizations representing nearly every industry. Our hope is that, through this book, you, too, will learn new ways to strengthen your culture and raise the collective energy and performance of everyone with whom you work.

ACKNOWLEDGMENTS

We would like to thank our clients, colleagues, and families for their insights, collaboration, and support, without which this book would not be possible.

INTRODUCTION
ENERGIZING A CHANGING
WORKPLACE

Picture Walt Disney World. We are standing in the Magic Kingdom, and the grand parade that takes place every day is rolling past. The parade has been exciting and entertaining, full of genuinely magical spectacles, and here at the end, heading toward us right now, is the final float, the one that excites the children more than any other. Here comes Mickey Mouse.

With this book, that's not what interests us. We could not possibly quantify the particular magic of Mickey Mouse. Many have tried that already, and we are not sure anyone has quite succeeded. Mickey is simply magic incarnate, we suppose. No, what interests us with this book is the guy coming up behind Mickey's float. We're interested not in the cast member who occupies that Mickey suit, but rather in the one who cleans up after the horse that pulls Mickey's carriage.

This is a true story. We knew a Magic Kingdom Parade cast member whose job was to follow Mickey Mouse's horse-drawn coach, which is always the last float in the procession of the daily three o'clock parade at the Magic Kingdom. This means that this one cast member was the last person anyone saw in the parade. His job? To shovel the horses' poop into a large can he pushed around on wheels.

So here's an employee who gets to parade in front of thousands of people every day as he winds his way through the Magic Kingdom, and he's doing it all with that rancid-smelling bucket rolling along at his side. If that had been us, we might have had a hard time getting enthusiastic about the role—never mind engagement. We would have been looking for a new job pretty much from the moment that first parade ended on our first day. This particular cast member, though, always had a smile on his face. He was so committed to the magic that is Disney World and the joy that it brought to so many people that he didn't just believe, but *knew* that every scoop he shoveled into his bucket was a key part of keeping that magic alive. He wasn't shoveling horse poop; he was making magic.

With this book, we are going to be discussing engagement strategies for today and tomorrow's workplace. And as leaders of organizations, the kind of engagement we strive for in every one of our employees should be exactly the kind of engagement we saw in that Disney cast member shoveling horse manure. That level of engagement is the surest way to bring perpetually positive energy to the workplace. It energizes everyone around you. It leads to commitment and loyalty. It causes the organization to retain more of its high-level talent. It helps develop lesser performers into workers that can make a more positive and lasting impact. It improves a staff's effectiveness from top to bottom. And if it works for someone whose job is literally to shovel horse dung into a bucket, then it can and will work for any role in any organization.

Blink, and Your Staff Has Changed

Think about the dynamics of the people and teams you have worked with recently. You may have noticed an interesting, if not troubling, trend: These days, the workforce on which we depend changes rapidly. People leave their employers for new opportunities more frequently than ever before. More and more often, organizations find themselves committing the time and resources to train a new employee, only to see him underperform or even depart before ever making a meaningful impact. Often, this leads to an underlying drain on the energy and commitment of an entire staff.

To succeed in this remarkably fluid new workplace, the best organizations must find ways to invigorate their staffs. That invigoration comes with a new focus on the importance of managers and the critical role they play in employee engagement and retention.

These trends are no accident. The rate of turnover from the retiring baby boomers to the millennial generation is almost unprecedented. Five million millennials enter the job market every year, bringing with them all the values, habits, and expectations unique to their background. The challenge that so many leaders face is how to energize a workforce whose needs seem to evolve and change from one day to the next.

Another part of the difficulty is in understanding and bridging cultural differences. Younger workers in the twenty-first century value different things than the stalwarts nearing the twilight of their careers. On top of that, you have the constantly advancing (and often disruptive) march of technological development. Myriad tasks have become automated, dramatically shifting workflows and rendering obsolete what used to be key roles. Throw in each individual employee's preferences for mode of communication, the spectrum of his or her expectations for how and when each might advance with a promotion, and the increasingly public manner in which social media allows us to lead our personal and professional lives. Add it all up, and we find that managers at every level often feel as if they are drinking from a veritable firehose of data. It can be all too difficult for them to keep up with changing demands, shifting staffs, and objectives that often feel like moving targets.

Although the pressures related to maintaining a hardworking and loyal workforce are nothing new, employers both large and small have recently begun to think about employee retention in a revolutionary new way. It all started during the so-called "war for talent" that came with the technology boom of the late 1990s. When the tech bubble burst, it left a vacuum of talent and created an incredibly volatile job market. Through it all, the organizations that found the greatest success were those that thought of employee engagement and retention not as a matter for the human resources (HR) department but as a *deliberate business strategy*. They saw that investing in the energization of their workforce improved productivity, managerial effectiveness, customer satisfaction, and the bottom line *across the board.*

We have used the word *engagement* a couple of times already, so we should take a moment to define it. Engagement is that level an employee reaches when she is ultimately committed to the organization, the leader, and the tasks at hand. An engaged employee brings discretionary effort to the job. She is passionate about the work, yes, but more importantly, she puts in the extra effort and thought that opens up new meaning in the tasks she performs every day. This employee doesn't simply do the work; she contributes to a larger purpose for the organization.

Embracing the Data (and Everything After)

We are well past the tipping point in our knowledge of the impact an engaged workforce can have on sustained organizational performance and success. Engaged employees act like caffeine for an organization—a java-crew that can enliven people around them, inspire creativity, promote high performance, and delight customers. You already know that, and most executives agree with you. It's no surprise that, today, 82% of all organizations make engagement a strategic priority, with over one-third of them ranking it among their top talent initiatives.

Trends tend to ebb and flow. Our workforce always seems to be in flux, with unemployment rates falling and rising in step with economic cycles. However, the impact that millennials are having, and will have, in shaping the future of work will be with us for a long time. Over the past year, millennials managed to overtake the baby boomers as America's largest generation in the workforce. The millennial generation comes with its own particular motivations and challenges, which we will get into later in the book. Perhaps the most recognizable characteristic of millennials is their connectedness, always exchanging information on a variety of mobile devices. Surprisingly, despite these motivations and challenges, less than 25% of all organizations use social media as an aid to connect with employees, build commitment, and promote retention. Not surprisingly, the exception is a best-in-class group of employers, where 55% have integrated social media in some form to assist their engagement and retention efforts.

Another unusual trend: For the first time in the twelve-year history of the TalentKeepers engagement-and-retention study known as *Workplace America*, the area most impacted by low engagement and high turnover was reportedly "Morale and Culture." There is no question that employers who work hard to energize workers, create opportunity for growth, and build pride enjoy stronger business results and achieve greater long-term success. But for those that fail or never even try the resulting downward spiral can be dire. One executive who completed this year's survey ended it by saying, "These questions have scared me."

Yes, more organizations are finding ways to generate, analyze, and use data to guide talent-management practices. The majority of them understand that employee data is the third leg of the key metrics stool. That's why, in 2016, employee surveys were the most popular and effective way of gathering relevant and actionable data on employee engagement. The problem isn't that organizations are refusing to collect data. The problem is that too many leaders with access to this data never wind up doing anything with it. This still boggles our minds, that even after organizations expend all the time and resources it takes to survey their staffs—after all the analysis, presentations, and discussions—they don't ask their leaders to do anything about it.

Applying workplace data is what we intend to explore with this book. We'll make the case for how the data can work for your organization, but more importantly, we'll make the case for your leaders' incredibly important role in using this data to improve engagement and retention and, as a result, to improve every aspect of the organization. In a major study we undertook earlier this year that included over 30,000 employees, those employees who believed their leader took some action as a result of the survey were 11% more engaged on every index we measured. The impact this has on business metrics can't be understated. Let's figure out how to make that happen for your organization.

The Confluence of Generations

All the talk lately has been about baby boomers and millennials, but consider this: The most senior members of generation X are turning fifty. In just ten years, they'll be nearing retirement age even as the last of the baby boomers are stepping down from work. This leaves millennials—the focus of so much hyperbole both complimentary and critical—as the largest, most diverse, and best educated generation yet.

A key question as we move forward is this: How well is your organization managing these three diverse generations? Where you work, are you witnessing a coalition of the generations or a collision of them? Perhaps, more importantly, has your organization begun to adapt to the incoming workforce? If you're a millennial, is your organization doing a good job creating the kind of workplace that's exciting, hard working, and one you would recommend to your friends? Based on our most recent studies, the likely answer for most of you is no. After all, only 40% of all organizations are providing their leaders with training on how to manage the millennials. At the same time, training for millennial leaders on how to tailor their leadership practices to gen X and boomers is, well, hard to find.

This slow growth in preparing leaders to better manage millennial employees is not due to a lack of knowledge. Eighty percent of organizations believe their leaders are, in fact, challenged by managing employees of different generations. Even the best in class report that their leaders are similarly challenged by this blending of three generations in the workplace, with 91% admitting to this challenge.

The millennial generation is the future of every organization. Major change is equally inevitable. But this doesn't mean we need to drastically change immediately. Rather, we can slowly adapt in ways that appeal to all generations with continual benefit for the bottom line. One of our survey respondents added that, "Open communication, autonomy, purpose, and mastery will be huge in engagement and motivation." We could not agree more.

"Begging Them to Stay"

That was one response when we asked for a description of the best strategy for managing employee retention. Although that may sound jokingly desperate, it speaks to what many employers are feeling. Organizations of all sizes are regrettably getting worse at retaining employees overall and, in particular, at keeping high performers. Only 15% describe themselves as "very effective" in retaining their best employees, whereas 36% are "not at all effective" or only "slightly effective" at retaining employees.

It's well understood that opportunity alone does not drive turnover, but it is a big factor. In fact, "job and career" issues have been the top reasons organizations have been losing people since the great recession began to ease in 2011. This overtook "ineffective leaders," which had long been the top reason people moved on. Most recently, however, leaders are increasingly a key stimulus for turnover. With that in mind, it will be important for us to figure out how to shift your organization's focus toward improving leadership practices.

Good Leadership Still Wins

This year's *Workplace America* survey has once again reminded us of the importance of leaders on employee engagement and retention. How well are leaders doing? Sixty-one percent of organizations believe that their leaders are at least moderately effective in their impact on employee engagement, with 15% having leaders that are very effective at energizing their workers.

Everybody knows that good communication is essential to promoting a healthy and productive workplace culture. This core interpersonal skill is at the top of the list of leadership development initiatives that, if improved, would have the greatest organizational benefit. Leaders are getting more effective at explaining the "why" behind organizational changes to their teams, highlighting the importance of effective communication between leaders and their employees.

Communication is the lubricant of an engaging workplace culture; silence is the friction. One of the best-in-class organizations said it well. When asked to describe the most successful employee engagement and retention tactic they used, this executive was clear: We require "monthly staff meetings, open communication, and transparency at all levels" of our business. All of that flows from the leaders to the staff. This makes leaders the most important factors in implementing your engagement and retention strategy. In the coming chapters, we're going to outline some strategies on exactly how (and why) this works.

Building a Winning Strategy

"I didn't realize how bleak things were until I answered these questions," said one executive in response to a follow-up query we asked regarding the study. If things really are bleak, "begging people to stay," as one participant wisecracked, may be your best, last-ditch play. But we all know it is better to focus on proven strategies and tactics that align with your priorities—strategies and tactics that attack the pain points, fit your budget, and can be embraced by your culture.

There is no magic solution or one-size-fits-all approach. The rewards of improved results and a vibrant work environment that come with high engagement and retention can only increase over time through the sustained execution of effective strategies.

How do we ensure that happens for your organization? How do you keep talented people motivated and engaged in this rapidly evolving environment? If you're asking these questions, then you've come to the right book.

1 Engaging Your Talent Is a Business Imperative

Kristen was running early. She felt upbeat, and not just from the skinny latte warming her cup holder. Until recently, her job had been a dull, unsatisfying slog. But today, not even the traffic clogging her commute on this cloudy and chilly morning could break her excitement about getting to work.

It had been ten months since she first made the decision to pursue that new position, and even though it was a lateral move with no pay increase, she found that it invigorated her in ways she never could have expected. At first she figured it was just the newness of the role that had her so energized. But the more time passed, the more she realized that she owed much of it to her new supervisor.

He was so different from anyone who had ever managed her before. He listened. He got to know her. He seemed to take a genuine interest in her success. When coaching her, he used specific examples that helped her envision what skilled performance looked like. In so doing, he earned her trust, which helped diminish the anxiety of learning a new job, asking for help, or voicing her opinion. She no longer feared being criticized or demeaned if she didn't immediately grasp a new task. It all felt so much more *constructive*. She was optimistic about her future, and it showed in her effort and enthusiasm.

Of course it's not exactly revolutionary to say that leaders play a pivotal role in energizing and keeping valued workers like Kristen. That's why it's so strange to learn that most organizations aren't doing enough to leverage the influence their leaders have on their employees. We will get to the data in a moment, but for now, let's put it this way: Where you work, how many engaged and energized people like Kristen are there? Equally important, what would it mean to your organization if more leaders were like Kristen's supervisor? What would that do for morale? For productivity? For your ability to meet defined outcomes? For your chances to innovate? For your bottom line?

When it comes to keeping and engaging high-performing employees, it's no longer enough to leave the responsibility in the hands of the HR department, as well-intended as they may be. The misconception is that employee engagement is a human resources "thing." But in truth, retention and engagement are *business* strategies with clear business outcomes. Of course, engagement and retention are supported by HR in many and varied ways, but ultimately these strategies and outcomes must be owned by the operations leaders in your organization. An engaged workforce positively impacts the customer experience, which improves employee/customer relationships, and, in turn, generates more revenue.

It runs deeper than that, as well. According to Debbie Weaver, a human resources representative from Stillwater Mining Company based in Billings, Montana, engaged employees are also *safer* employees. Stillwater mines palladium as their primary product, with platinum running in second place. With hundreds of employees working irregular shifts inside hundreds of miles of subterranean tunnels, the company tends to see its share of employee turnover. Part of that owes to the notion that it's difficult enough finding people willing to work

11.5-hour days for four consecutive days before four days off. Then throw in the idea that these same people must next take a shift where it's five nights on, followed by five nights off. Rotating hours aren't for everybody, and the pliable sleep schedule tends to bring engagement issues bubbling to the surface.

"Engaged employees are more productive," she said. "The higher our levels of engagement, the better our production numbers. But for us, the biggest thing we have seen is that there is a direct correlation between engaged employees and how they view safety." Every metric made available to Stillwater showed that their more engaged employees believed safety was a priority for the company, and for their leaders. That top-down view of the importance of safety has driven home a safer and more engaged environment, which has, in turn, allowed the company to take steps toward decreasing turnover rates.

Imagine a truck set to drive down into a palladium mine. That truck has a brake light out. While driving the roads above the surface, that might seem like a minor issue, but if you have an accident inside a mine, the stakes tend to rise considerably. An engaged employee is more likely to recognize that brake light issue and immediately report it to the driver and to a supervisor who can do something about it. Meanwhile, someone who simply shows up to "do his job" might not care enough to help avert potential disaster. The *business* difference between the two can be immeasurable—it's the difference between all the lost productivity during an accident, plus the cost of repairing the truck and replacing the damaged load versus avoiding the disaster before it even happens.

The same holds true for everything a company can value. Engaged employees deliver better business results across the board. Think about the last time you walked into a retail store that was full of employees who didn't seem to have any real interest in helping you learn about the product and answer your questions. Did you buy that day or just head out and order on Amazon instead? Conversely, how much more willing have you been in the past to buy from an employee who is genuinely engaged with her job and intent on an-swering your questions? John F. Kennedy once said that "a rising tide lifts all boats." As you increase engagement, every business measure rises with it.

"When your staff feels engaged, they take ownership for the organization," says Donna Fayko, director of the department of social services in North Carolina's Rowan County. "That ownership shows up in the quality of service they provide to customers, which obvi-ously is a huge part of any organization's success."

By now, it should be no secret: We believe that the effort to en-gage and retain talent must move out to the front lines. It must rest squarely in the hands of leaders like you. We have seen it time and time again: When leaders hold themselves accountable for energiz-ing their most talented employees, every aspect of the organization improves. Great leaders are, beyond a doubt, the most effective strat-egy for enhancing organizational success. The more talent you keep and engage, the better you perform across the board.

So how do you keep and engage your best workers? Some might suggest competitive pay, comprehensive benefits, flexible work sched-ules, and even team-building programs. While these measures are in-deed helpful, they are not enough on their own. The effort takes great leaders. It takes leaders with a well-honed skill in building a climate of engagement and retention—a climate that speaks to employees in a way that encourages them to get connected and do their best. These leaders are an organization's best defense against turnover, poor performance, and a host of other workplace ills. They are the not-so-secret weapons in keeping valued contributors actively engaged and in hanging on to them longer.

For all these reasons, we posit a simple premise for this book: If you want to improve your organization, the process starts and ends with your leaders. Again, this stance is not necessarily revolutionary. Many books extol the impact of leaders. What makes the strategies we offer in the coming pages different is that they stand on sixteen years of data compiled from thousands of companies of all backgrounds and goals and in any industry you can think of. Thanks to this data, we have assembled a strategy for shaping people in management positions into leaders that have the exact same kind of impact on their employees' careers, as Kristen's did on hers. The results speak for themselves. Every organization that has embraced and executed these strategies has seen significant improvement in all measures. We look forward to unlocking this same potential for yours.

The True Cost of Turnover

Keeping and engaging talent is such a valuable organizational tool for many reasons, but one of the most often overlooked is that staff turnover is so costly. Not only does keeping your best employees ensure that your teams are more productive, innovative, engaged, and just plain good at what they do, it also improves the bottom line dramatically. Cutting the cost of turnover puts more dollars back into the budget, improves return on investment, and allows you to focus more energy and capital on more productive interventions.

Your organization likely already expends time and resources on determining where it can control and minimize cost in an effort to increase profits. Thus, the fact that so few organizations make this same effort to identify and minimize the cost of employee turnover is surprising. In fact, many major industries such as retail, fast-food restaurants, call centers, and construction simply assume high turnover is an inevitable part of the business. Maybe the reason is because so many leaders have come to accept the unfortunate idea that high turnover is something they can't control. They accept that, when the market is loose, finding and training employees is less expensive, and that in competitive markets, skilled and talented job seekers are scarcer, which often raises costs. That does not have to be the case. An organization that commits to keeping and engaging more of their talent can avoid fishing in these turbulent waters, and more importantly, cut the huge costs associated with replacing key employees.

Of course the points we mention above don't apply to *everyone*. Many organizations do take the steps necessary. They compile the data on the direct costs of turnover and use it to their advantage. In their view, the effort is so simple and straightforward that it doesn't make sense to ignore it. So they identify and calculate the expenses associated with recruiting; interviewing; training; purchasing new equipment, tools, and uniforms; and so on. Well-run organizations also identify the costs of efforts like exit interviews, expenses like separation pay, and increases in unemployment tax, the payroll that must be allocated to temporary help or overtime, the time and money that goes into orientation processes, and more. But what too many organizations fail to account for are the (often hidden) indirect costs as well.

Think about the last time a valued member of your team retired or left for another job. What happened in the aftermath? The short answer is that you lost productivity, time, and a great deal more money than you may realize. When a key member of your staff leaves, productivity almost always suffers as you try to transition from a talented and knowledgeable employee to one who is still learning the ropes. Then you have the financial impact of lost revenue from lower sales when a seasoned salesperson resigns. Your organization also experiences the inevitable drop in customer service and overall customer experience, which threatens loyalty and a customer's willingness to recommend the business to friends and family.

Usually, morale takes a hit, too. A working relationship shares at least that one key similarity to any other personal relationship: When someone you care about and/or count on leaves, you tend to miss them. That is true of the departed employee's coworkers and any customer he may have interacted with as well. According to our research, stress levels rise, team performance declines, service quality suffers, and everyone finds themselves having to spend at least some measure of time picking up the pieces of team morale and organizational culture.

When assessing indirect costs of employee turnover, also consider the lost revenue from the open position. We must think about the total number of workdays the new hire will need before she reaches total effectiveness. That ramp-up time, commonly known as time-to-productivity, can be remarkably costly. Then, attrition of other jobs might result from that frontline employee's departure. You can see the ripple effect at play here.

All this takes a toll on the bottom line, a toll that most organizations fail to account for. Our national research suggests that only 23% of organizations are aware of the direct cost of attrition of frontline employees, and fewer still, 10%, know the indirect costs, which are typically even higher. So what is the true cost of turnover? The answer may surprise you. The data we have collected shows that the average direct cost of losing a valued individual contributor is nearly $17,000. The added indirect cost is just over $26,000, bringing the total replacement cost to $43,000. It is important to keep in mind that these are just averages. For your organization, the number could be higher or lower. For example, in a cost-of-turnover study of forty-two contact centers, both in house and outsourced, the average cost of losing an experienced agent is $8,780. As a general rule of thumb, the true cost of replacing an experienced frontline employee is one-half to one times their annual compensation. For a frontline leader or manager, the cost doubles to one to two times their annual compensation or more.

This is why it is so important to estimate both the direct and indirect costs of employee turnover as a gauge not only of financial impact but also of morale, team performance, and so on. Knowing this cost is not only the first step in the effort to reduce such costs and improve profits, but also the first step in justifying the investment in high-quality leadership and other tactics that effectively engage and keep your best employees.

Interconnected Spheres

Patti McEwen is a career HR manager who worked for a wide
variety of companies like Frito-Lay, Atari, and DHL before
arriving in her current role with Sheridan Healthcare. Given
that this was her first time working in healthcare, she found
herself having to adapt quickly to the particular rigors of a
physician practice management company. The similarities
to what she observed in her former roles were clear, but
the variability from practice to practice served as a unique
challenge. Her role went from figuring out how to engage
roles and teams within a single corporate sphere to learning
how to engage interconnected but largely unrelated spheres of
specialty physician practices.

Sheridan has contracts with hospitals all over the country,
creating the relationship between healthcare providers and
physician groups that provide specialty services like anesthesia,
neonatology, and radiology under the Sheridan umbrella.
The company has six thousand employees, two thousand of
whom are doctors, two thousand of whom are nurses, and
two thousand of whom are medical support staff. All six
thousand of these employees fall into one of hundreds of
different specialty physician practices that serve one (or more)
of dozens of hospitals and clinics all over the country. With an
organization like that, it's obviously difficult to know exactly
what engages this varied group of employees and adheres them
to the overarching culture of Sheridan.

"We decided that our best strategy would be to conduct
a survey with the physicians that lead each practice,"
McEwen told us. "Our goal was to identify what engaged our

physicians the most, and also what really motivated them to stay with Sheridan." So McEwen worked with TalentKeepers to implement a survey to highlight the factors at play. "The highest scores for engagement were the location, camaraderie, and the people they worked with," McEwen explained. "But the one that stood out to us was the leadership component. It was less important for the physicians to feel like they had great leadership from the more remote leaders at the corporate level. They didn't feel as connected to or motivated by the corporate side as we would have liked."

This proved to be a bit of a disappointment for McEwen and her team, but not surprising because the physician groups Sheridan engages with were typically working as their own autonomous practices before joining the Sheridan family. They related more directly to where and to whom they went to work with every day than they did with the organization that supported them from the top down. After the initial training period ended, it was often difficult to maintain that connection between parent organization and daily practice.

"The survey showed us that most of our physician leaders were effective at the local level in terms of driving engagement, but less effective at providing Sheridan leadership related to our corporate programs and initiatives. They operated in their own smaller spheres, in other words." The opportunity, as McEwen saw it, was to connect these spheres with Sheridan. "It's one thing to say, 'We're changing your timekeeping system tomorrow and you have to follow a whole new workflow,' and a much better thing to be able to tell them how, when, and why this is happening, and how it will benefit them. That was a big gap for us to have to bridge."

(continued)

Interconnected Spheres (cont'd)

What McEwen and her team figured out is that the leader is critically important to the initiative. "Our leaders have four roles to play," she said. "The medical role they're obviously good at. It's what they have studied, trained, and worked for over the course of many years. Quality of care is obviously their top goal on this front. Second, at the local level, they have to manage their staff (doctors and nurses) and the Sheridan staff that handles the administrative and HR side. The third key role is to manage the financial success of the practice. The fourth piece is leadership and interaction with the hospital or clinic site and the leadership staff at that particular facility. In other words, the success of this leader is huge for the business and for Sheridan because that leader is the face of everything we do."

Given all these factors, finding physicians who can manage all of this is often challenging. They must lead a successful practice and serve as the face of Sheridan at the local level. For Sheridan, finding, promoting, and engaging such leaders is a clear market advantage.

Leadership as a Market Advantage

For over eighteen years, we have worked for a company that essentially created the employee retention market. During that time, we have encountered a glaring fact that still surprises us. Out of the thousands of organizations we have worked with on engagement and retention strategies, we continue to find that leaders—particularly frontline leaders—remain the most underutilized resource.

In the 2018 edition of *Workplace America*,[1] the longest continuously running national study of employee engagement and retention trends, we found that 44% of all US companies reported that "leadership strategies" would have the greatest impact on improving retention. So we know that many companies at least value the impact their leaders can make. That the number is only 44% is a little startling, but at least a somewhat significant percentage of people recognize the importance of what we are dealing with here.[2]

The same 2018 research confirmed that importance. Improved leadership strategies have the single greatest impact on engagement. On every team—no matter the level, the organization, or the industry—*leaders* set the tone. They choose what information to share. They interpret company rules and how to apply them. They reinforce and coach. They are the face of the company to their employees. So why aren't more organizations leveraging their leaders in a more significant way? Why is it that the top two obstacles to meeting business goals are (1) lack of employee longevity and loyalty, and (2) lack of adequate leadership?[3]

Hello! These two results are linked. They are also well understood. Yet so few companies are doing anything about them. According to our *Workplace America* research, a mere 31% of all organizations reported that they required leaders and their team members to conduct quarterly one-on-one meetings to discuss engagement topics. In stark contrast are best-in-class organizations, where 70% require these meetings at least quarterly. A shocking 19% of non-best-in-class organizations *never* asked leaders to meet formally with employees in an effort to boost their engagement and encourage them to stay.

As part of the study, we assessed nearly every incentive that could boost the performance of frontline employees. Raising pay, offering better benefits, providing additional job-specific training, and on and on—leader effectiveness trumped them all. In spite of that, more than half of all organizations (54%) do not allocate the necessary resources for leadership development in the area of engagement and retention.

You don't want to be like them. In this changing organizational climate, with high turnover as we transition from the baby boomer to the millennial generation, we are looking at a new and extremely valuable trend: Organizations that leverage their leaders to engage and retain employees achieve a significant advantage. When it comes to talent, this is the new market inefficiency. And this market inefficiency, like any others, offers plenty of opportunity for those who take action.

Introducing the Leader Engagement Index

In an effort to uncover the reasons that employees underperform, are less engaged, or even decide to leave, companies often invest the time and resources it takes to determine the best ways to improve morale, productivity, and employee satisfaction. What savvy companies have learned is that the source for many of the best ideas and tactics is hiding in plain sight: the employees themselves. To find these best ideas and tactics, they ask the people who work for them every day.

Organizations that choose to formalize their employee survey processes benefit from key insights that help them improve. Many of them work with outside experts to boost survey participation by ensuring confidentiality and to compare themselves to benchmarks with others in the same industry. In addition to these advantages, employee surveys provide the following additional benefits: (1) prove to employees that the organization cares, (2) provide a basis for accountability and action, and (3) offer a sounding board for everyone, no matter their role.

Since our data shows that leaders are the most important factor when it comes to keeping and engaging employees, and since we know that employee surveys are effective on all the fronts listed in the preceding paragraph, one of the most effective strategies an organization can implement is to survey its employees on their opinions about their leaders. This is why the Leadership Engagement Index (LEI) is such a powerful tool.

Put in its simplest terms, the LEI is a composite of the data gathered from multiple behavioral questions presented to an organization's employees. The results are expressed as the percentage of team members who are currently engaged by their immediate leader. Imagine being able to see how all leaders within your organization vary, from 100% to 0%, on LEI. Imagine the power of comparing the LEI score with team performance (almost always a strong positive correlation) as a way to demonstrate the value of leader engagement on performance. Organizations who successfully do this find that they have a new lever to pull to drive higher performance: the power of highly engaging leaders. Perhaps even more exciting is the ability to show leaders with lower LEI scores the exact behaviors they can modify to increase their LEI, and in turn, their team's performance. Data from the behavioral questions comprising the LEI provide actionable information for all leaders tasked with improving leadership engagement.

With all the frenetic energy buzzing around HR metrics these days, the LEI is the *key* metric tied to employee engagement. Nothing is more valuable when it comes to assessing a leader's effectiveness in motivating and inspiring employees. Thanks to the sixteen years of data we have compiled on hundreds of thousands of leaders, we have extraordinary insight into the behaviors that lead to the most direct and complete understanding of the engagement and effectiveness of any leader. The LEI is the surest means to compare leaders on the most important thing they do: *lead*.

So how does it work? Every leader's employees receive a survey that asks them to rate their leader on statements like these:

My supervisor wants me to be successful.

My supervisor uses specific work examples while coaching me.

My supervisor enables me to achieve the career and professional goals I have set.

My supervisor is usually receptive regarding suggestions from my employees.

My supervisor communicates effectively.

I am satisfied with the recognition I receive from my supervisor for my achievements.

The feedback and coaching my supervisor provides me helps me improve my performance.

My supervisor is someone I can trust.

Once each employee has provided answers to the twenty-two statements similar to the eight listed above, the data gets compiled into a percentage. The higher the percentage, the higher the engagement; the lower the percentage, the lower the engagement. Importantly, we have also found a direct correlation between high Leader Engagement and high performance from the teams they lead. The same is true of low engagement correlating to low performance.

We have generated an extraordinary amount of data from thousands of organizations over the years, and these are the ones that shine the brightest light on job performance. A high LEI score almost always leads to high job performance, specifically in areas related to customer satisfaction. What is more, for cases in which we find high engagement scores on underperforming teams, the data can show us exactly where the shortfalls are happening. In most cases, it means the leader is liked and respected but doesn't hold his teams (or himself) accountable for meeting goals, policies, or procedures. Conversely, a leader with a low engagement score but a high performing team achieving good operational results might be holding her team members accountable for all the right things, but not in a way that the team likes, respects, or appreciates. Although these kinds of situations can benefit the organization in the short term, ideally these leaders will eventually shift toward practices centered on engagement.

This leads to the next great value that LEI provides: The organization can conduct this measure as often as it sees fit. The index is not a static number. It can (and should) be tracked over time. A lower performing leader might achieve better numbers during the next survey, thanks to newly embraced engagement practices. Leaders with a high LEI score one year might find their scores dipping in the next. The scores provide excellent insight not only into senior management but also into the frontline leaders and employees as well. Senior leaders identify which of their managers needs more training or better strategies for engaging their staff. Frontline leaders get to see the specific areas in which their leadership might be lacking. Employees get the sense that their employer cares enough about them and trusts them enough to honestly assess their leaders and serve as the impetus for change.

As you can see, the survey results can be incredibly valuable. They help an organization identify underengaged and unengaging leaders while also finding solutions to make their inconsistent results more consistent. The effort to reshape leadership toward engagement strategies ultimately strengthens the organization from top to bottom.

In the chapters to come, we will be discussing exactly how you can use the LEI to create real results through your leaders across the organization, but for now, let's examine the core principles that the index can instill in your leaders and the people they lead. They are:

Trust Builder: Highly engaging leaders build trust between themselves and their team members. A trusting relationship frees employees to be more creative, be more open to coaching and feedback, feel more comfortable offering ideas, and communicate more openly.

Communicator: These leaders proactively and thoughtfully share information to keep team members, helping them to be "in the know," an essential for high performance and retention. They keep team members informed, involved, and fully engaged in their work; and help employees know how important information affects them.

Esteem Builder: These great leaders focus on building esteem and pride in their team members. They have an attitude of gratitude; empower individuals to be responsible for their own work; show appreciation for the team member's contributions; provide time for individual attention.

Flexibility Expert: An engaged leader is flexible in recognizing, understanding, and adapting to individual needs and views. This leader respects the need for greater flexibility in the workplace, such as offering flexible work schedules or allowing team members to work from home.

Developer and Coach: These leaders fuel professional growth by providing training and coaching that allows employees to develop new knowledge and skills. They understand the benefit of targeted behavioral feedback; they help employees uncover and pursue opportunities to use their talents and develop personal competence that contributes to professional growth through varied and challenging work.

High-Performance Builder: Engaging leaders will conduct performance-building exercises to reinforce high levels of team member performance. They align performance objectives; recognize and respond to performance opportunities quickly; and push employees to stretch themselves and exceed their expectations, but in a constructive and supportive way.

Climate Builder: These leaders create a work environment where individuals form cohesive and collaborative relationships based on team spirit that involves everyone feeling like a part of the group. They encourage creativity, originality, and enthusiasm, and inject energy and fun into the workplace.

Generation Manager: Outstanding leaders orchestrate the diverse talents, styles, knowledge, and experiences reflective of the three major generations in the workplace: millennials, generation X, and baby boomers.

Talent Finder: Great leaders recruit individuals that fit specific job characteristics. They match individuals with work that showcases most of his or her natural talents; make every effort to add the best person possible; use current top performers as a recruiting resource.

Retention Expert: These leaders foster relationships with team members, are aware of changes in their engagement and satisfaction, and take proactive steps to address issues. They understand talents, skills, and abilities of top performers and the cost of replacing a valued contributor; connect people to broader company goals; make team members feel part of something meaningful. These leaders acknowledge that individuals have different abilities, personalities, and aspirations.

These principles all contribute to creating an environment in which employees see the value of their work and a connection between their success and the success of the organization. See Figure 1.1 for

Case Study

	Leadership Skills
1 Highest	**Trust Builder**
2	**Communicator**
3	**Talent Developer and Coach**
4	**Retention Expert**
5	Climate Builder
6	Flexibility Expert
7	High-Performance Builder
8	Esteem Builder
9	Talent Finder
10 Lowest	Generation Manager

Figure 1.1 Leadership skills most valued by employees.

Source: First Fit Survey, Q4 through to Q1 (N = 16,039).

a rank order of how these leadership skills are valued by employees. The key to creating a culture of engagement is employees recognizing that their performance and contributions genuinely matter to the organization.

Further, these principles are exactly why Kristen finds so much more satisfaction in her job these days. During her morning drive, it all began to crystalize for her. Yes, she thought, there was a lot to like about her new leader. It really came down to the relationship he patiently and deliberately built with her during those early months. Her new supervisor's ability to earn her trust, keep her informed, develop and coach her, and build her self-esteem reignited pent-up energy while diminishing the anxiety of learning new skills, voicing an opinion, asking for help, and growing into her new job. Kristen's story is one of many that prove how, with a focus on leader engagement, *everybody* wins—employees, supervisors, and the organization at large.

Notes

1. *Workplace America: Employee Engagement and Retention Trends*, TalentKeepers, 2004–2018.
2. Ibid.
3. *Workforce 2020: The Looming Talent Crisis*, Oxford Economics, working with technology firm SAP, 2014.

2 What Engages People at Work?

Three employees from a major communications conglomerate sit down to complete a survey about their engagement with work. First we have Mike, a member of the baby-boomer generation. He has worked for the company for nearly twenty years after an earlier career as an insurance agent. Mike works as a middle manager at a call center that fields technical support requests.

Then we have Janet, a member of generation X, whose employment with the company began seven years ago. Janet works as an associate attorney in the legal department.

Finally, there is Justin, a graphic designer for the marketing department. Justin is a member of generation Y, and has been with the company for just under two years.

We asked all three employees to provide responses to the same four statements/questions:

1. Describe the one thing that most influences you to stay with the organization.
2. Describe one thing that could cause you to leave the organization.

3. What would increase your willingness to recommend, to a friend or colleague, your organization as a good place to work?

4. What would increase your willingness to recommend the products and services your organization offers?

We will delve more deeply into Mike, Janet, and Justin's specific answers later in the chapter, but for now, let's keep in mind three important trends that have emerged from the millions of answers we have compiled through surveys like this one: (1) There are four key drivers of employee engagement (organizational factors, job/ career satisfaction, coworker relationships, and credible leadership); (2) different generations tend to favor those four drivers in slightly different ways; and most importantly, (3) no matter what generation, organization, or industry we're talking about, quality of leadership is the absolute most controllable driver of employee engagement. There is nothing that an organization can change quicker, easier, and to greater results than how their leaders approach employee engagement. Put simply, if you want to engage and retain the most employees possible, the absolute best place to start is with your leadership.

The Tipping Point

Before we address the four drivers, let's take a quick look at a few statistics that highlight how important engagement is as a business imperative that should be prioritized, managed, measured, and reported like many other key performance indicators, like most companies do for customer satisfaction. A growing number of major studies reinforce what the most successful executives have long understood: Engaged workers perform better, stay longer, and deliver greater results—and the numbers bear it out.

It all starts with a study of recent history. Over the past ten years, we have seen a tipping point emerge. US companies once enjoyed the heady boom times of growth fueled by the real estate bubble. Then they got knocked down and dragged through the deepest recession since the 1930s. Lately, most of these companies have regained their footing and now have a new outlook on what it takes to succeed in the twenty-first century. At the time of this writing, unemployment has dipped below 4%, and job growth is stronger than it has been in many years. The best organizations realize that now is the time to capture this momentum and ensure that their workforce carries the organization forward.

Meanwhile, a decade ago, millennials barely registered on the employment radar. Now, at roughly ninety-five million strong, they are a welcome wave of smart, energetic labor. On the other hand, they may be a disruptive force made up of workers impatient with the workplace status quo and driven by unrealistic expectations.

Increased competition in many industries—from banking and retail to transportation and entertainment—demands a renewed focus on the customer experience. Engaged, experienced employees are proving to be a key weapon in raising customer satisfaction, average transaction value, and brand loyalty. As a result, budgeting for these efforts has slowly gained traction, with 61% of US organizations reporting that they budget funds for these initiatives. Figure 2.1 shows the percentage of organizations budgeting resources for employee

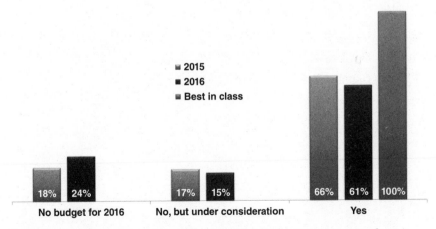

Figure 2.1 The percentage of organizations budgeting resources for employee engagement in 2015 and 2016.

engagement for the past two years. The latest analysis shows that these organizations have seen a dramatic impact on operations and sales metrics and a measurable return on investment.

It should come as no surprise that employee engagement is now a strategic priority for 82% of US companies. For our best-in-class group of employers (the top 10% of all participating firms in engaging and retaining employees), 100% of them make engagement a priority and budget funds to support key initiatives. More on this important point in Chapter 3.

Best-in-class organizations continue to innovate, trying new strategies and tactics to weave engagement more deeply into the fabric of their businesses. Most often, it is the leaders of these organizations who direct and implement these initiatives. They employ deliberate strategies facilitated by clear goals and accountability throughout all levels of leadership, with links to key performance indicators in sales, customer satisfaction, and operations, and reinforced through incentives.

Award Your Best Asset

Budget Director Bertha Johnson shared with us a unique perspective of her staff with the government of the city of Durham, North Carolina. She explained that, absent a product or service to sell, the local government's *employees* are their most important asset. They are, after all, the ones who interact with the client and project the most direct picture of the organization's quality. "We recognized early on the importance of employee satisfaction," she told us. "Employees that are motivated and engaged are more likely to be innovative and proactive in their jobs. They don't wait for someone else to fix a problem; they solve it independently. They also tend to be more efficient and productive, which allows a tax-funded organization like ours to do more with less."

To get to the desired level of engagement, Johnson's group began by working with employees to identify the organization's core values, including them in the new employee orientation process, and listing them in many highly visible places throughout the offices (including on every employee badge). Next, they implemented employee recognition and empowerment programs like DurhamFirst, a committee of volunteer employees tasked with leading and coordinating organization-wide development efforts. On a monthly basis, they recognize what they call their "STAR" employees (Show and Tell Award Recipient), or those people who best exemplify the organization's core values. Award recipients are chosen by their peers via email or handwritten nominations. "The program allows us to tell the untold stories of our employees," she said. "It lets others know that their work is appreciated, and thanks them for what they do. There's tremendous power in that."

The results speak for themselves. At Durham, greater employee engagement has led to higher service, quality, and productivity, which, in turn, has led to rapidly increasing resident satisfaction with employees, and with the community as a whole.

I Don't Need No Satisfaction

Job satisfaction is a wonderful thing. An employee who is satisfied with his job is happy with environmental factors like workspace, pay, employment location, benefits, and on and on. People who are satisfied with their jobs tend to have little to complain about when it comes to the day-to-day operations of how they get to work, how they are compensated for that work, and what they must do in order to receive that compensation. A satisfied employee's observations about these elements of his job tend to fit closely with his expectations and standards about those same elements.

For all these reasons, an organization must strive for the highest possible job satisfaction for every employee. Engagement, however, is something that runs much deeper than satisfaction and, as a bonus, is often far more controllable. This is because people factors are what control and drive engagement. Engaged employees feel supported, inspired, motivated, and coached by their leaders. Engaged employees are internally motivated, inspired to contribute discretionary effort, and make a difference at work (for customers, coworkers, and the organization). They are committed to making a difference, and if they have a leader who reinforces and fuels their engagement, they *excel* over time.

Inspired employee

Stillwater Mining Company, an organization that used to face high levels of attrition related to job satisfaction, looked at whether they were hiring the right people for their particularly unique environment. They called the program "Hiring for Attitude." It involved presenting a more realistic job preview, where they took prospective employees on a tour of the mine, made it clearer that shifts would span a full 11.5 hours and rotate on a four days on, four days off basis. Rotating hours aren't for everybody, obviously, but sometimes simply delivering that message was all they needed to overcome a preventable loss.

At six, twelve, and eighteen months, Stillwater now interviews their hires for feedback, asking direct questions about what is working for them and what could be improved. "We found that improving engagement was just as simple as improving our signage underground," Debbie Weaver told us. "We have a hundred miles of roadway down there. Sometimes morale with new hires would suffer just because they didn't have a clear idea of how to get around."

After performing these surveys, they determined that the organization needed a leadership development program to help extend a sense of ownership and advancement to more levels than just frontline leadership. The program focuses on specific qualities the

organization values in a leader, and each leader-driv[e]
on one of these qualities. "So far, feedback has been ...
Weaver said. "We've put a hundred people through the program
a couple hundred more to go." And even though the process is not yet
complete, Stillwater has gone from 36% turnover in the first eighteen
months of the employee life cycle down to less than 10%.

So in a nutshell, satisfaction is great. It is about an employee's self-
perception of status compared to her "happiness" with her surround-
ings. But engagement is where the true power lies, because it is what
drives employee behavior.

The Four Drivers of Employee Engagement

As we mentioned in the introduction to this chapter, the four drivers
of employee engagement are (1) organizational factors, (2) job/
career satisfaction, (3) coworker relationships, and (4) credible
leadership. Figure 2.2 illustrates these four engagement drivers and the

Figure 2.2 The four engagement drivers and the performance outcomes
they produce.

performance outcomes they produce. Let's take a look at each driver before determining the most logical course of action for most organizations seeking to increase engagement and retention of their employees.

Organizational Factors

Organizational factors include perception of senior management, the organization's vision and mission, reputation, policies and procedures, culture, and environment.

An engaged employee tends to make these kinds of statements about the organizational factors that contribute to her job:

The organization's vision, mission, and goals inspire me and help me to be more productive.

Senior management in my organization is open, honest, and transparent in communication.

Senior management is accessible and approachable when necessary.

I feel that I can question a policy or practice without fear of being penalized.

My organization's policies and procedures help create an effective work environment.

My organization consistently demonstrates that delivering customer value is a high priority.

My organization's process and procedures to evaluate and promote employees is fair.

My organization shows respect for employees.

My organization supports a balance between work and personal life.

I am satisfied with the location where I come to work on a daily basis, and am also satisfied with my commute to work.

As you can see, many of the preceding points reference how an employee feels she "fits" into the organization in question. Because there are so many different (and often unchangeable) factors related to that "fit," the organizational driver can be more time consuming and costly to address. It is one thing to reshape an organization's vision, mission, and goals—or more appropriately, to improve the message that helps your employees connect to the vision, mission, and goals—and entirely another to consider moving the location of your offices to better suit employee engagement.

This is not to downplay the importance of the organizational driver, which, along with the job/career satisfaction driver, show up often in employee surveys as primary factors that motivate their engagement.

Job/Career Satisfaction

The components of job/career satisfaction include clarity of job roles, job responsibilities, accountability for goals, opportunities to utilize skills, and chances for career growth. Although the overarching trends in US employment have been positive of late, unfortunately not all news is good these days. For the third consecutive year, job and career issues have sparked more turnover and lower engagement than any of the other four drivers, including having a lousy boss (which has long been the top reason people reported they quit).

It all boils down to whether the employee likes what he does, feels as if he is using his skills and can learn new skills, sees an impact beyond the task at hand, and, most important, finds meaning in his work. An engaged employee tends to make these kinds of statements about the job/career satisfaction measures that contribute to his job:

My decision-making authority is sufficient for me to perform my job effectively.

I receive the training needed to perform my job effectively.

I have the information and resources needed to effectively get my work done.

At work, I have the opportunity to utilize my skills and do what I do best.

This is a career that I love and believe in.

I am satisfied with the tasks and responsibilities associated with my job.

At work, I have sufficient opportunities for personal and professional growth.

My job is challenging and interesting.

I am satisfied with the benefits my current job provides.

I am satisfied with my current work schedule.

I fully understand my compensation plan.

My compensation is proportional to the contributions I make.

We mentioned how, over the past three years, these factors have had a greater impact on turnover than the other three drivers. TalentKeepers has been tracking and reporting on this trend for over a decade, and at this point, it's clear that we must look at this as something other than just a short-term phenomenon. It appears that, as we transition to a greater number of millennials in the workforce, job/career satisfaction has become more and more important. And factors associated with the job itself need greater focus. Leaders still play a huge role in stay-or-leave decisions, and can greatly influence how people feel about their jobs, but organizations must pay more attention to job and career growth issues. The opportunity to learn new skills, do things they do well, and see a path forward—all are important to retaining people and keeping them engaged.

Fortunately, much of this connects to how leaders approach their relationships with their employees, so the initiative ties in well with our focus on leadership. More on this in a moment.

Coworker Relationships

Our third driver relates to the people with whom we work. Team-based relationships, including peer support and everyday work interactions, can make or break how satisfied an employee feels, while playing a key role in overall engagement.

In the traditional corporation of the past, commitment was a matter of the bond between an employee and the company. People felt a loyalty to their employers. As long as a company took care of its employees, they could expect implicit commitment from those same employees. Unfortunately, gone are the days when companies were able to offer the same level of job security they could in the past. As a result, the new organization can expect its employees to form an attachment not to the organization itself, but rather, to the employee's own job or team. Today's employees (and in particular, millennials), take their sense of worth from their projects, opportunities, and affiliation with others rather than a bond with a particular company.

What is driving this change? Research shows that people pull together when they are faced with some kind of common threat. The economic conditions in the last decade have caused employees to have to face the perils of downsizing, takeovers, mergers, and negative reactions among team members affected by feelings of apprehension, uncertainty, and resentment. Employees who previously may have been a loose working group with little in common now recognize the kinds of pressures that they can't quite understand or manage directly. In these situations, new bonds form as team members unite to attack the things they can manage, and take comfort in what they do have in common. As a result, stronger bonds form among coworkers.

The stronger these bonds, the more engaged an employee becomes. Here are a few examples of statements an engaged employee might make:

Most of my coworkers communicate effectively with me.

From most of my coworkers, I receive the support I need to be able to succeed.

Most of my coworkers demonstrate interest and concern for my personal well-being.

While working on assigned tasks, most of my coworkers do not just participate, but rather, seem engaged with the work.

Most of my coworkers deliver quality work and put forth extra effort to help our organization succeed.

Most of my coworkers value and support my work and career goals.

It is no secret that coworker relationships have become important to modern employees, but the trouble is that ensuring that positive coworker relationships form is difficult. The only truly effective strategy is to foster these relationships from the leadership structure down. In other words, like the other drivers, how your leadership performs and interacts with their employees is crucially important. Only leadership can create a sense of belonging for each employee, build mutual trust and commitment among the staff, and make the workplace more enjoyable and satisfying. This is a huge part of why we save the most important driver for last.

Credible Leadership

Here is where we can make the greatest difference as leaders of an organization. Credible leadership involves engagement of team members by immediate managers, including communication, trust, coaching, and recognition. Leaders are the lens through which employees see nearly everything. Their behavior has a significant impact on the workplace experience of their team members. They shape expectations, set the mood, deflate or energize, coach and develop (or smother), empower, and incent.

Here is what a leader who effectively engages her employees looks like:

Tells the truth, meets commitments, and does what she says she will do.

Is someone an employee can trust.

Listens when an employee has suggestions on how to do things better.

Clearly communicates expectations and the reasons behind changing priorities.

Provides feedback that helps employees improve their performance.

Serves as an effective coach and motivator who enables employees to achieve their career and professional objectives.

Empowers employees and creates an environment that encourages decision-making.

Recognizes individual efforts and achievements and wants each employee to be successful.

Makes work challenging and satisfying by encouraging fun, and provides as much choice as possible regarding work activities.

Increases each employee's desire to come to work and do her best.

Is interested in having only the best-qualified people added to the team.

Demonstrates concern for a new team member's fit with the organization's values, goals, and practices, as well as how likely they are to stay with the organization.

Recognizes and takes into account everyone's work/life balance needs.

Provides flexibility and choice in how each employee does his work.

Holds team members appropriately accountable for performance.

Supports high goals, keeps employees informed of progress, and emphasizes how their work contributes to organizational success.

Believes an engaged and stable workforce is important for organizational success.

Is aware of team members who may be thinking of leaving, taking appropriate action to encourage them to stay.

Identifies top performers and creates ways to engage and retain them.

Adapts his or her communication and coaching style to effectively relate to younger workers.

Remains sensitive to generational differences in the workplace and responds appropriately.

There are many business reasons to make leaders the best strategic and tactical resource to drive engagement and retention. Based on our years of research, best-in-class employers clearly view their leaders and their role in engagement highly. They understand that they must involve leaders in engagement strategies. A leader is entrusted with developing a team, after all. Since these organizations already provide leadership training, they simply review the curriculum and determine if the mix of topics addresses engagement and retention skills like building trust and having growth conversations with each employee.

Leaders are already held accountable for a variety of metrics; a retention goal and team engagement metric helps reinforce the importance of engaging employees. These metrics should tie into an incentive or bonus in the leader's compensation plan. Further, if you already evaluate your leaders each year for the succession plan, you can make engagement and retention effectiveness an essential criteria for consideration. However you approach the subject, leveraging your leaders to engage your employees is a highly effective business strategy for any organization. So let's move on to discuss how to make that happen.

The Four Drivers and the Leadership Engagement Index

We return to the model with which we opened the book: the Leadership Engagement Index (LEI). The concept starts with the notion that you understand that some leaders are better than others at engaging their team members. The LEI helps you determine which leaders are strong with engagement and which could use some work, which then helps you establish strategies for raising the numbers across the board.

Why is this important? Because leaders are the deliverers of information from the top down in any organization. The four drivers are all important, but leaders stand to make the most positive change. We know that the leader has an impact on employee perceptions at work. Compensation is the perfect example. People either think it's fair and competitive or they think they're underpaid. Of course, part of that has to do with the actual monetary value, but at TalentKeepers, we have also seen two organizations with the exact same compensation plan, one whose employees were satisfied with their pay and one whose employees were not. What was the difference? The way leadership talked about, positioned, and supported the compensation plan.

Across the board, leaders with a high LEI talking about compensation and all the other drivers made a huge difference. If a leader with a high LEI talks positively about the compensation plan, his team reports being happy with that plan. If a leader with a low LEI talks down on the compensation plan (saying things like, "I don't know what HR is thinking; I agree with you; we need more money"), then it shouldn't be a surprise when the team reports dissatisfaction with the plan.

Obviously the job/career satisfaction driver still applies here. We can't ignore the amount of pay entirely in this equation, after all. If pay is unreasonably low, a leader with a high LEI has to work that much harder to keep her team engaged. But if pay is at least reasonably competitive and fair, how a leader talks about it can make all the difference.

In a large customer service organization, we compared employee perceptions of pay to individual leaders' LEI. Fifty supervisors managed teams that averaged about twenty customer service representatives each. We compared each leader's LEI to their team's perception of their pay, which was identical across all fifty teams. Those leaders with a high LEI had team members consistently rating their compensation as more competitive and fair than those leaders with a low LEI. How the leader treats employees, and specifically how they talk about pay, can shape employee perceptions.

And pay is only one component. LEI correlates positively to all the other factors listed in the four drivers model outlined earlier. A leader with a high LEI score can influence and shape an employee's perception of team building, career opportunity, self-esteem, sense of self-worth, safety, and on and on. On this note, the business case for holding leaders accountable for building engagement on their teams is clear: High LEI leaders generate engaged employees who perform better in any role, which drives stronger performance and results in sales, customer experience, productivity, and so on.

For Mike, Janet, and Justin, the answers to the questions on the four drivers were varied. Asked what one thing would increase their willingness to recommend their organization as a good place to work to a friend or colleague, their answers trended toward matters related to scheduling and compensation. More flexible hours and higher pay and better benefits ruled the day with these respondents, as well as with the millions of employees who have taken our surveys over the years. The answers to "What would increase your willingness to recommend the products and services your organization offers?" trended toward matters related to better communication and more thorough understanding. But with the first two questions on the four drivers, the picture on leadership began to emerge.

Baby boomer Mike's "one thing that influences you most to stay within the organization" was, "My chief values very highly my contribution to the practice, and provides me with the time and material to conduct my practice correctly." For gen-Xer Janet, the answer was, "Upper management listens and takes care of problems right then and there. I am very satisfied with corporate support." And for Justin the millennial, the answer revolved around "excellent leadership of the department."

These kinds of answers are consistent across the board in every survey we have ever conducted. When it comes to a desire to stay with an organization, leadership is the most important factor. Great leaders with high LEI scores generate more engaged employees, which leads to better employee retention. Conversely, Mike, Janet, Justin, and the millions of others who submitted responses also pointed to a lack of leadership as the "one thing that could cause you to leave the organization."

Leaders can make or break a workforce. The time to invest in their ability to make a greater impact is now.

3 Leaders and Their Impact

We recently facilitated a leadership development program for a large cable television operation in the upper Midwest. During that time, we had the occasion to meet a supervisor named Madison. At the ripe old age of twenty-three, Madison's new supervisory role was one of the first jobs she ever held out of college, and by the time we met her, she had only been working in the role for six months. Naturally, this meant that she spent much of the morning with that deer-in-the-headlights look so familiar to many training professionals. So during the first break, I sought her out and initiated a conversation.

"I'm curious, Madison," I said to her, "how prepared do you feel for this new leadership role of yours?"

"Truthfully?" she said. "I don't feel at all prepared."

She went on to describe all the technical and operations training she had received as a new leader, and while she thought that was helpful, she also believed that it lacked in the kind of guidance and skill-building she needed to handle the wide array of individual and team situations that a leader is expected to handle. Even employee issues as straightforward as repeated tardiness created a challenge for her. How should she handle something like that with someone who once was her peer? Never mind the time she had to address another team member who made an emotional outburst about the unfair way that the leadership team determined work schedules.

"The transition has been a little jarring," she explained. It was easy to see how that could be the case. She had recently moved from being a friend and colleague of her team members to now being bombarded with performance, attendance, and other personnel issues as their leader.

As Madison and I were chatting, I happened to notice an experienced supervisor named Manny sitting alone in the back of the room. His participation and contributions during the session had impressed me. To me, this seemed like a golden opportunity.

It turned out that Manny and Madison knew each other as colleagues, but not well. I sat us all down together and asked Manny to share some stories of the challenges he faced as a new leader. With every story, Madison seemed to grow more comfortable that she wasn't in way over her head. Next, I asked Manny to describe for Madison all the key information and insights that most contributed to his transition to leadership. Manny was happy to oblige.

The two of them talked throughout the break, and later worked together in a small group that met frequently during the workshop. Afterward, Madison shared with me that this was the best and most helpful training she had participated in since her promotion.

On a return visit to the site three months later, I learned that Madison had transitioned so well to the role that she was one of the highest scorers on the company's LEI surveys. Not only had she gotten comfortable with her new role, but she had learned how to excel at it.

So what is the lesson here? The surface lesson is that this simple combination of formal training, peer coaching, and the sharing of best practices will go a long way toward helping the Madisons in your organization find success. The deeper message that we will explore with this chapter is that the investment in time, energy, and resources will provide a *huge* return on investment compared to the cost of failure. As we have been saying, investing in leadership is the surest, quickest, and most complete business strategy on which an organization can focus.

With this chapter, we present a simple challenge: Let's make sure we are paving a clear path for our leaders. For new leaders, we need to ensure that they know *how* to be a competent leader. We can't assume that they naturally know how to drive team performance forward (at least not without using authority or intimidation in their leadership style). For existing leaders, we need to have programs and messages in place that help foster their growth as leaders and commitment to the organization.

The Case for a Focus on Leadership

Many new leaders fail to excel in their new roles. They rely on technical competence or operational knowledge to guide them. But new leaders quickly find themselves faced with a plethora of "people issues" that they are unprepared for and uncomfortable addressing for fear of wading into waters too deep for their skills. New leaders unprepared for the role will craft ways to dodge people-related squabbles, challenges, and even coaching opportunities. Soon, employees become disenchanted, engagement falls, attrition increases, and performance wanes. Unfortunately, this is a well-traveled path.

According to Jim Bowles, former vice president of workforce development at Cingular and then later at AT&T Wireless, leaders are the driving force of any engagement and retention initiative, but they're all too often unprepared to lead in this way. "Broader buy-in is what leaders can deliver," Bowles told us. "It's not just enough that the person's direct manager understands how to apply these tools. Within the organization, from the front line up to the highest levels, a focus on leadership increases the chances that this kind of initiative will be successful. If everybody is talking the same language and applying the same specific engagement strategies, then reinforcing it at every turn, then it all works far better."

At AT&T, Bowles observed this effect throughout the organizational hierarchy. It usually started with a manager who had a blind spot about why this effort is so important. If a leader has spent his whole career focusing on delivering the desired business numbers, it's sometimes tough to get her to put in the work to create better relationships with the staff. "But they would always become a believer once they saw how these tools work," Bowles said. "Leaders have so many things coming at them in terms of the metrics they have to manage, the numbers they have to meet, and the sales they have to make. Sometimes engagement strategy falls down the list of priorities. We found that it was up to upper management to drive this up the priority list. Then, every time there was follow-through, it would show tremendous results. Then it would catch on like wildfire."

Supervisors are the face of the company for the majority of employees in most organizations. Recognizing that leaders, particularly those on the front line, play a starring role in retention is only the first step. No leader comes to work wanting to do things badly. But desire and motivation alone do not beget skill. Leaders need to be trained in key skills and understand their role in retaining and motivating people. Leadership development must be about specific business outcomes, and few business priorities will have more visibility in the near future than keeping talented employees and ensuring that they're actively engaged in their work.

When it all works, when an organization zeroes in on helping leaders learn how to be retention experts, you get quotes like this one from a customer service representative in a TalentKeepers study: "My current manager is supportive, flexible, caring, creative, knowledgeable, sincere, and focused. She carefully develops a personal relationship with our entire team. Her dedication and support has been unsurpassed. I can honestly say that I love her for her caring drive and desire to ensure our success as a team. She's a true professional in her commitment to excellence, and her desire to succeed. She's honest in her dealings, and a trusted leader. I have the greatest respect for her as a true leader; what an asset to this organization. Let's clone her and watch our company grow with creativity, enthusiasm, and excitement as we take the marketplace by storm!"

HR is likely to gladly share ownership of this initiative. But good planning and sound implementation are necessary to help leaders embrace their part in retention, not to mention the need for them to learn new skills and behaviors. In order to hold leaders accountable, providing them the training and support to perform their new role is a critical success factor. Surprisingly, given the mountain of available research on leadership skills covering everything from vision and strategy to delegation and feedback, precious little has specifically targeted retention, one of the most costly of all business problems.

Why Focusing on Leaders Gets Results

In the previous chapter, our discussion of the four drivers of employee engagement and retention highlighted an important (and all too often overlooked) point: Leaders are the one driver that can change the quickest in terms of their influence on engagement. From a leadership perspective, it's all about awareness of the engagement issue and the leader's behavior in relation to the initiative. Hopefully no leaders come to work and say things like, "How do I break trust today?" or "How do I let my team down today?" And yet too many leaders are unaware of the little things they do that have that same impact.

The impact of leaders on all of the other engagement drivers is so significant that we created a model to illustrate the impact leaders have on organizational engagement. Figure 3.1 charts the relationship between leader engagement and organizational engagement and identifies four types of team member sentiments that result. The descriptions that follow of the characteristics of leaders and teams within each of the four quadrants will hold true most of the time. However, there are always exceptions to look for when determining the best way to coach a leader in each of these areas.

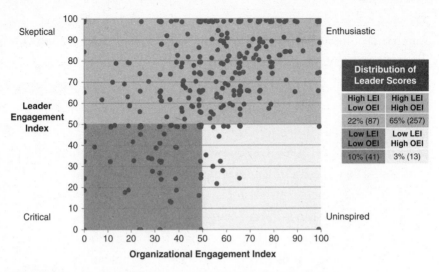

Figure 3.1   Leaders' impact on organizational engagement.

Enthusiasts

When both leader and organizational engagement are high, employees are enthusiastic about their leader and the organization, they're engaged, and they're likely to be strong advocates for the organization and its leaders from top to bottom. Your goal should be to fill your organization with these types of leaders and teams. Recognize these leaders for their ability to engage their teams just as you would any other performance metric. "Pick their brains" to understand how they are creating such favorable impressions of the organizational engagement elements. Perhaps you will discover some best practices you can leverage with other leaders and groups that are not performing as well. Sharing this data among leaders can help reduce the rationalization that some lower-performing leaders may have that every leader must be struggling with these issues. Seeing peers with much stronger results can get underperforming leaders to ask themselves how they can modify their leadership approach to better engage their teams.

Skeptics

When leader engagement is high but organizational engagement is low, employees like their leaders but are skeptical about the organization and senior leadership. Consequently, these teams tend to hesitate before adopting change because they're not sure the change is positive or whether it will indeed stick. This makes it difficult for the organization to quickly pivot in different directions to be more competitive and effective. Often, these impressions of the organizational engagement elements are colored by how the immediate leader is describing them. Commonly, leaders who have teams that are skeptical about the organization are "blaming up" when it comes to discussing issues to which their teams are reacting negatively, such as changes in goals, policies, procedures, and so on. We will talk more about the blaming-up behavior and its negative impacts on the organization and the leader in Chapter 4. For now, understand that these leaders can greatly improve their teams' organizational engagement by helping them understand the reason behind decisions and providing favorable insight into the leadership teams above them.

That said, one of our clients reminded us there are other factors besides leaders blaming up that create skeptics. Organizational change puts stress on communication channels within the organization, particularly at the front-line leader level, which is why we often explore whether these leaders are blaming up. When rapid-fire organizational changes like restructuring departments, moving key leaders to new roles, or revisions to policies that affect many employees, they feel the strain. If senior leadership is not effectively sharing the "why" behind these changes to lower levels of leadership, these leaders are not able to be advocates for the decision, leaving them unable to confidently reinforce and support changes. Senior leaders on many levels should include a "sharing down" strategy to enable all levels of leadership to support and communicate the changes. Top management also must recognize that there are limits on how much change employees can tolerate. At some point, key employees will begin to assess whether or not their professional and personal goals still align with an ever-changing environment and may consider moving to a more stable organization.

Critics

When both leader engagement and organizational engagement are low, employees are likely to be critical of their leader, the organization, and senior leadership. You must help these leaders and teams improve their engagement, or you risk having their negativity spread to other teams. Examining the elements that comprise the leader and organizational engagement factors and identifying those that are particularly high and low is a good place to start. Leverage the more highly rated elements as positives upon which you can build broader constructive sentiment. Utilize the lower-rated elements as opportunities to learn more from the team members about what the leader and organization could "Start, Stop, and Continue" doing to improve. Consistently and sincerely asking these questions takes the pressure off the leader to guess on how to improve and encourages team members to think about these elements with a "how can we improve this?" attitude. Ultimately, the engagement levels of these leaders and teams needs to be improved; or instead, consider where there may a better fit for them elsewhere in the organization.

Uninspired

When leader engagement is low and organizational engagement is high, employees are often satisfied with the organization as a whole but are not giving that discretionary effort so sought after by engagement efforts. If leaders can leverage employees' affinity for the organization and inspire them to contribute more, then these teams represent an opportunity. Focusing on the lower-rated leader engagement elements is a proven method for improvement. Employing the "Start, Stop, and Continue" questioning sequence is especially effective here, because all the elements within the leader engagement driver are firmly within the control of the leader.

With the proper awareness, great leaders begin to identify those behaviors that are preventing them from being seen as more engaging by their teams. It's often a subtle change—not a watershed one. A leader can adapt and change in small ways to make a huge difference. For this reason (and many others) the leadership driver can generate positive and quick change. That's good news for organizations. It's tough to change the organizational drivers quickly, likewise, the job/career and coworker drivers. But leaders are a different story.

According to our colleague Dr. Richard Vosburgh—who is well versed on employee engagement practices, having held senior leadership roles in organizations including MGM, Compaq, Campbell's Soup, and Volkswagen—the data proves that employee satisfaction leads to customer satisfaction, which, in turn, leads to improved financial outcomes. Vosburgh has dramatically improved engagement for a number of companies, but while working with a large and fast-growing technology firm, he proved this correlation with empirical data. His research established the relationship between employee and customer satisfaction, customer satisfaction and both gross margin and market share, employee/customer satisfaction with brand equity and shareholder value, and more. In other words, as Vosburgh explained, "Talented, motivated, and empowered employees find better operational ways to deliver results, allow us to meet and exceed customer expectations, resulting in the delivery of our financial commitments."

Another major component of why this is true is that leaders are the lens through which their teams view everything else about the organization. In the *Workplace America* research, we ask a question about how frequently leaders meet with team members to talk not just about performance or the status of a given project but also specifically about engagement. Meetings about engagement involve questions like, "How are you feeling about your role here? Are you achieving what you want in your career? Am I doing what you need to achieve your top performance? Am I recognizing you appropriately and giving you proper respect for what you do?"

In our studies, we have found that 70% of the best-in-class organizations have these kinds of meetings at least quarterly. Twenty-six percent of those same organizations conduct these meetings as frequently as monthly. On the flip side, some organizations (19%) never have this meeting—ever. This is a huge oversight, as a leader has so much power to shape the employee's views of the organization. The more a leader focuses on discussing the individual employee's needs, the more the individual employee feels engaged and willing to stay. The more often these meetings happen, the better—and the effort leads to spectacular improvement in business results, almost across the board. Figure 3.2 depicts the big difference between best-in-class organizations and all others on this important metric.

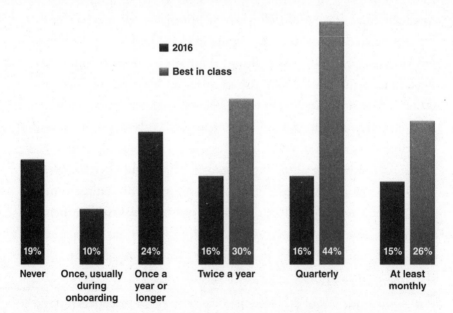

Figure 3.2   How often organizations have meetings about engagement with their employees.

Since leaders have the most interactions, observations, and dialogue with employees, this makes them the best person to talk about the employee's career and coaching. Our research shows that more leaders could be having these conversations. It's no fault of theirs, though. Most of them aren't aware it's part of their job. Others don't want to make a mistake like overpromising to a team member that they're going to get a promotion or a raise or training/development or anything they would value from a career standpoint because the leader isn't sure whether promising such things is feasible, appropriate, or even within their authority.

Unfortunately, this compels some leaders to avoid giving honest feedback to their underperforming team members. We see a lot of career frustration on the part of employees in part because they don't receive that direct feedback. It's far easier for a leader to tell a team member that they're doing great and are on the list for being recommended for promotion. It's not as easy to have the more difficult conversation about what's preventing you from being considered for advancement. This is something that more leaders are going to have to work on in order to improve engagement for their employees.

Finally, focusing on leaders gets results because those leaders already have the responsibility to improve employee engagement. Many of them just don't realize that fact. Reinforcing that it *is* part of their job to improve engagement is the quickest way to achieve the result you desire. Only they can make team members feel engaged, important, valued, and so on. If you ask team members what they like about their leader, for the best leaders they begin with statements like, "They have my back." If the employee needs something or they make a mistake, they know that the leader will be their advocate. These kinds of leaders drive engagement, not just in themselves and in their team members, but in other leaders as well.

Those leaders that have found a way to get better engagement from their teams often hold the key to how other leaders can achieve the same success. The real opportunity is to look at leaders who have been able to achieve high LEI scores and share this data with lesser performing leaders. When you're working with an engagement initiative and you're assessing, don't hide the data. Comparing and contrasting performance on engagement and retention items is important so leaders can learn from their peers who are doing well.

Best Boss/Worst Boss

We know that leaders and their approach to leading *directly* affects employee perceptions of many major organizational factors, such as job and career growth, compensation, culture, teamwork, and more. Data shows that an improvement in leadership strategies will have the greatest impact on employee engagement, as reported by organizations that have participated in our *Workplace America* research. According to those same organizations, improving leaders' communication skills will have the greatest impact, followed by increasing their ability to effectively coach and develop their teams. Figure 3.3 shows the percentage of organizations that see each engagement factor that,

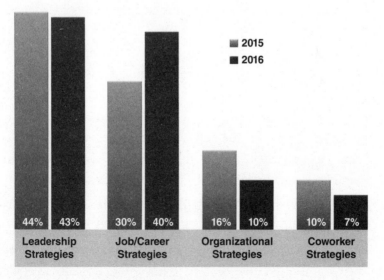

Figure 3.3   Impact of improving each engagement factor.

if improved, would have the biggest impact. Note that job/career strategies are seen as most impactful by a growing percentage of organizations. This suggests that the most impactful strategy would be to leverage the leader as a conduit for career discussions with employees. We'll say more about this in Chapter 5.

It's obvious why this is the case. Everyone knows the old adage "people don't quit companies, they quit bosses." Think about the best boss you've ever had. What were some of his qualities as a leader? As a colleague? As a human being? Now think about the worst boss you've ever had and ponder the same questions.

We have done exactly that with millions of survey respondents and in hundreds of workshops. We have asked participants in our surveys—some of them leaders, some of them in non-leadership positions—to think of the worst boss they have ever had, and toss out a word that describes them. Every time, we get a long list of statements like, "He was condescending," "He was a micromanager," "She was never available," "He was untrustworthy," "She was overly critical," and on and on.

When discussing this lousy boss, we would present questions like:

"How excited were you on the drive in to work every day?"

"How willing were you to go the extra mile for that leader?"

"How badly did you want to quit or transfer?"

"How did this leader impact team morale?"

And so on. You can imagine the negativity in the responses. In a nutshell, excitement was low, as was morale and willingness to work hard. People working for someone they identified as a bad boss expressed an active interest in finding a new job far more often than their counterparts working for a good boss.

When you pose these same questions to these same people, asking them about the best boss they have ever had, the contrast becomes clear. That kind of leader's impact runs deep. It affects people's engagement, energy, motivation, trust, loyalty to the organization, self-esteem, performance, and so on. The Leadership Engagement Index returns similar numbers every time: Best bosses retain higher numbers of employees and keep them engaged; worst bosses underperform. How the bosses go, so goes the business of the organization.

So we know that leaders matter most. The question is, why don't more organizations understand the value here? Further, why don't more leaders embrace the idea that, to improve their teams, they must improve the way they interact with those teams?

We're going to dig deeper into these questions in a moment, but for now, keep this in mind: It's not about the money. Sure, if you pay your leaders more, you may get better people seeking leadership roles, but money only takes you so far. Across the board, we have found that improving the quality of leadership is more about raising awareness around three issues:

1. Leaders matter more than they realize when it comes to employee engagement and retention.

2. Employees from different backgrounds respond in different ways to different sorts of interaction.

3. The focus needs to be on improving every employee's progress through what we call the "commit, engage, excel" continuum.

Leaders Underestimate Their Impact

Leaders—particularly frontline leaders who interact with the greatest number of employees—routinely discount the influence they have on their team members' engagement and retention decisions. This reaction is not defensive or a rationalization, either. After training tens of thousands of leaders, we believe that they are genuinely sincere in this humble belief. If we want to get leaders to be open to accepting their important role in the employee engagement and retention equation, then this is the first notion that we must dispel. But how?

One technique we successfully use in our leadership development programs is to ask leaders how influential they are on their team members' engagement and retention levels. Consistently, these frontline leaders place themselves in the bottom half of the top-ten influencing factors such as pay, schedule, benefits, promotion opportunities, and so on. We then ask another question, much later in the session, regarding the influence that their immediate leader has on their own engagement and retention. Consistently, these frontline leaders rate their manager as a top-two or top-three factor. We then ask why their own influence on their team members would be any less than their manager's influence on them. You can see the light bulbs flashing as they reassess their own influence.

This strategy is effective, but it comes with an important caveat: This message should be one of empowerment—not punitive accountability. When you build this increased awareness, most leaders are eager to learn how they can leverage this newfound influence to increase engagement, retention, and ultimately performance.

Ultimately, the best way to show leaders how much they impact their team members' engagement and retention decisions is to measure their influence through the LEI metric. This becomes more impactful when we show leaders how they compare to their peers on LEI, and the behavioral components that comprise the LEI metric. Many leaders with lower LEI scores get wide-eyed when viewing the LEI scores of their peer group. Suddenly, their perception that "everyone must be struggling with this" is turned upside down when they see that other leaders in the same role, dealing with the same challenges, have found a way to achieve higher scores. Most of the time, these higher LEI peers are also enjoying higher team-performance levels, which lead to more compensation and opportunities for growth. This "aha moment" often turns a skeptical leader, who blames everything and everyone but themselves for low engagement and higher turnover, into an interested learner looking to leverage their newfound influence.

Different Background, Different Response

Every organization depends on human beings to work together to achieve organizational success. But it's important to recognize that human beings always fall into subgroups with their own identifiable attributes. In the previous chapter, we introduced this topic when we referenced the differences between the baby boomer, generation X, and millennial generations. From an organizational standpoint, we must also separate high performers from the rest of the pack and engage with them differently. Paying attention to these kinds of sub-groupings helps an organization identify strategies that will increase its ability to engage and retain the most crucial and talented individuals, and to increase organizational success as a result.

The most important point to note is that specific subgroups have different motivations, work styles, job/career aspirations, and so on. Catering your engagement and retention efforts to fit those groups almost always proves beneficial.

The confluence of multiple generations in today's workforce makes it easy to see that knowing how to adapt leadership techniques to suit specific generations is a highly valuable leadership skill. When asked if their leaders are challenged by leading employees of different generations, a surprising 91% of organizations agreed. This is a leadership trend heading in the wrong direction, with 65% agreement in 2012 and only 39% in 2011. The millennials are likely the complicating factor, and their entry into the world of work is quickly growing.

Because of that (and since it's now the largest generation in American history), let's start with the millennials. Tech savvy, energetic, socially conscious, and hard working, millennials will soon make up half of the working-age population in the United States. Today, they make up 35% of the workforce, surpassing baby boomers in 2015 as the largest generation in the US workforce. They have a strong, pent-up desire to either get started or get on with their careers.

The millennial generation comes with its own styles and preferences that may prove difficult to understand for leaders who are not prepared for the change. Millennials tend to require precise instruction, frequent feedback and coaching, check-ins and praise, and transparency in communication. "We don't turn off," a millennial employee working at a technology firm once told us. The point here is clear. They are always connected—to business apps, blogs, Facebook, Twitter, Instagram, and on and on. For them, countless digital tethers connect them to the outside world. Social media isn't only social; it bleeds into the millennial lifestyle and work life. These approaches to work are often at odds with some of the more traditional leadership styles and workplace cultures. How organizations and their leaders respond will impact how engaged their millennial employees become, and how long they will stay with the organization.

Tenure Is the Best Medicine

When we spoke to Bruce Belfiore, a colleague of ours with BenchmarkPortal, a company that works with call centers looking to reduce turnover, he opened our eyes to an important and often overlooked benefit of having long-tenured employees. Through his company's survey-driven "Agent Voices" report, Belfiore revealed that long-tenured employees are happier with their jobs overall, and more satisfied with their work and lives. That's the intuitive part. The counterintuitive part is that, over the past few years, even at call centers where customer satisfaction has been rising overall, agent satisfaction has been

(continued)

Tenure Is the Best Medicine (cont'd)

falling. This struck Belfiore as strange, because those two categories had always seemed to move in tandem. But upon further analysis, the data showed that the divergence was due to the increase in use of automated self-service.

"Self-service has gotten so much better over the past several years," Belfiore explained. "These better automated systems are taking care of more and more of the easy questions that people working in call centers used to field." In other words, people working in call centers were once used to dealing with a higher percentage of calls that were easy to resolve. Now? "The more a call center relies on automated systems, the more of the easy calls get syphoned off through the interactive machine, and the tougher the calls the agents have to field."

With this changing tide, tenure and engagement become even more important, Belfiore told us. It's one thing when you spend half your day addressing simple matters that you can breeze through easily, but it takes an experienced and satisfied employee to face day after day of complicated customer service encounters. This is a huge part of why reducing turnover and creating more engaged, longer-tenured employees is such an essential component to organizational success.

A manager well trained in dealing with millennials knows the importance of adapting management practices to allow these team members to work hard and achieve their goals without sacrificing established practices of the organization. These managers show concern for the well-being of their team by allowing millennials to learn while they work, challenging them with work they find interesting, incorporating the use of new technology in their tasks, and using familiar language to make these members feel comfortable.

Millennial generation employees are very much aware of their career aspirations and opportunities, yet those aspirations don't always fit common career paths. Leaders of millennial employees need to be informed of career and job opportunities, and proactive but realistic when it comes to helping millennials evaluate personal career goals and how to achieve them. Adaptation and flexibility will be required on both sides of the career equation as this generation floods the workplace.

Another sound investment is to train leaders on how to effectively engage and retain millennial team members. Our research shows that this type of training is on the rise, but the majority of organizations (60%) are still not onboard. The bright exception is once again our best-in-class organizations, where 84% are providing this resource for their leaders. See Figure 3.4 for the trend on how this type of training is increasing.

In many organizations, millennials are now leaders. Madison from the cable company story at the beginning of the chapter is just

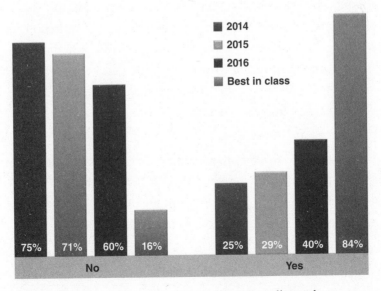

Figure 3.4   Training leaders to engage and retain millennials.

one of many examples. Millennials are now well into their twenties and thirties, which puts them at prime ages to begin accepting leadership roles. The burning question is, how do millennials engage and motivate boomers and generation Xers who work for or with them, either as employees or peers?

We're going to be discussing these key principles throughout the book. For now, let's turn our attention to another key group of employees: high performers. These are the highly valued, consistent contributors that give organizations a distinct advantage in today's marketplace. Engagement and retention of this group is a key piece of the performance puzzle.

High performers add value in a variety of ways. Often exceeding performance expectations and goals, they motivate and support those around them while contributing to a positive culture. They can improve the functionality of teams as a whole and can help to diagnose or even solve performance issues in low performers. This group of employees offers personalized feedback to colleagues, models commitment, and serves as an example to other team members of what it means to excel.

A sound investment in high performers is expected to provide a positive return. For the best-in-class organizations, 70% report having a strategy in place specifically for engaging and retaining high performers, and their results illustrate the benefit, because 100% of best-in-class organizations rate their organization as at least moderately effective at retaining their best contributors, with 35% rating their organization as very effective.

High performers often are recognized and reinforced for their contributions, but having an effective engagement strategy targeted specifically for them will go far in keeping this high-value group delivering results for your organization, instead of somewhere else.

So what is that effective engagement strategy? How can we engage different key performers and leaders from different backgrounds? It all starts with commit, engage, excel.

Commit, Engage, Excel

TalentKeepers has developed an engagement continuum that we use to describe the process of getting individuals engaged with their work. As you might have guessed from the title of this section, it's called "commit, engage, excel."

Many people think of engagement as a light switch that we turn on or off. We often think of people as either engaged in their work or not. In reality, becoming engaged in one's work is a process we all go through. Figure 3.5 illustrates the commit, engage, excel continuum.

Let's talk about the three phases of that process:

1. **Commit:** Each of us makes a commitment to our job in various ways and to different degrees. We commit to a role, a leader, the team, and the organization when we see alignment between what we want to achieve from our work and what we perceive the opportunity will provide to us. Employers want people to make intellectual, emotional, and even behavioral commitments to, for example, perform to the best of our ability. This commitment

Figure 3.5 Commit, engage, excel.

begins during the recruiting process and evolves as an employee gains more experience. This is why it is so important for recruiters to provide a realistic job preview to potential employees.

2. **Engage:** Once we make that conscious or perhaps subliminal commitment, we begin to dig in and apply ourselves. At this point, we have the opportunity to become engaged in the work and bring that energy and discretionary effort to our role and the organization. As we described earlier, the four drivers of engagement and retention play an important role here over time: credible leadership, supportive coworkers, job and career satisfaction, and a high-performing organization.

3. **Excel:** For many employees, engagement leads to sustained high performance over time, and we excel in our roles. Here is where all stakeholders—the employees, their leaders, and the organization—reap the rewards of discretionary effort in the form of higher performance in the areas of service, sales, productivity, safety, and so on.

As a reminder, employee engagement is the ultimate goal here because it improves employees' ability and willingness to contribute to organizational success, especially their willingness to give discretionary effort, going beyond what is typically required in their position to make the organization successful. Employee engagement is an essential element of organizational health. An engaged workforce leads to more committed employees, higher-performing individuals, satisfied and loyal customers, and a more productive and profitable organization.

So how do we get there? As the continuum suggests, it starts with commitment. Engaging your leaders to increase the commitment from their teams is a matter of communication. The process involves implementing a "stay interview," for example, and establishing a structured procedure for improving communication. Trust is also a building block in fostering commitment. Getting leaders and employees to connect and commit to each other, their roles, and the

organization is imperative for building engaged, loyal, and productive team members. Organizations that are successful in achieving this
goal enjoy the following benefits:

Stronger bonds between the leader and her team.

Commitment to the organization, the leader, and the role.

Quicker time to productivity.

Reduced early-tenure-turnover rates.

The next phase of the continuum, engage, calls for ensuring that
all the four drivers of engagement and retention are working effectively for your employees. Organizations with a highly engaged workforce
enjoy many advantages, including the following:

Committed employees

High-performing workforce

A productive and profitable organization

Satisfied and loyal customers

The final phase, excel, leads to a continuation of the development
of an engaged culture. By this point, leaders are focused specifically
on areas of engagement and are empowered to enhance interactions
and performance with team members.

Helping your employees adapt to new challenges and needs while
excelling in their roles is an ongoing challenge. Your organization
is invested in these employees and motivated to coach and develop
them to their fullest potential. Organizations that create this atmosphere enjoy the following outcomes:

Effectively manage change at all levels

Foster career growth, regardless of the trajectory

Avoid "quit and stay" and other plateauing behaviors

Guide high-performing individuals through transitions

Once we achieve a highly engaged workforce whose team members are excelling in their roles, the only thing that can derail us is the only true constant in life: change. When changes arise in an organization (the more typical kind of change being when a new leader or team member joins the organization, with the more rare being something like an acquisition or merger), a previously committed, engaged, and excelling team member needs to make a recommitment to the new leader, role, or organizational change. This recommitment is necessary for the employee to reassess whether this changed environment still aligns with their individual goals and aspirations. Changes to team members' personal situations—such as the birth of a child, caring for an aging parent, or attaining a college degree—will have the same impact. Employees experiencing personal change will need to reassess whether their role, leader, coworkers, and organization still align with their changed situation.

So how do we combat the impact of nearly constant organization and individual changes? First, we must understand the goals and aspirations of each team member through effective conversations and relationship building. Second, we must document this information for each team member, and refresh it periodically to capture changes to their individual goals and aspirations. Another benefit to documenting this information is that it will allow future leaders of the team members to build upon previous leaders' work versus having to start anew. And third, whenever an organizational change impacts an employee's commitment—a change in role, change in leader, change in a major policy—management needs to proactively communicate, through every leadership level, the reasons behind the change and the impact the change may have on team members' roles, leaders, coworkers, and the organization.

Because organizations are constantly changing, the next chapter will discuss strategies, tactics, and pitfalls for successfully maintaining a highly engaged culture in an ever-changing environment.

4 Communication: The Lubricant of Change

When we first began work with the Clerk of Courts office in Orange County, Florida, a major, unexpected change occurred. A week before they were scheduled to begin an organization-wide employee survey, the elected Clerk ofCourts passed away. They would not get another elected clerk into the leadership role for over one year, and they had two interim, unelected clerks before the next election. In other words, over that first year-plus that we worked with them, they saw more than their fair share of the disruption that change can render.

During that time, the office was experiencing significant breakdowns in trust throughout all levels of the organization. The results of the employee survey we were to help them run would have been quite useful to them at the time, but unfortunately, with the death of their leader, the data wound up being put on hold. When the new official took office, she came with a different vision about how to improve the organization, and the survey results remained idle indefinitely.

"We were just in this constant state of not being able to get settled," explained Steve Urquhart, HR strategist with the Orange

County Clerk of Courts. In an environment like this one, making sure the employees are settled is often a top priority. The vast majority of the employees with the organization serve in a clerical role, which means that any change to the process—whether procedural or technology based—tends to disrupt workflows and impact employee morale.

For example, their recent shift from a paper to a paperless workflow didn't only upset the processes the staff had relied upon for years; it completely changed the way the organization thought about how to manage their work. "It has had an impact on the organization because it requires you to think differently about the work and push more empowerment down to the frontline employees. A technological shift like this one stretches our functional capabilities, and many of our employees' comfort levels."

From the outside looking in, this kind of workflow change might seem like a trivial matter, but here we are talking about people who have been performing clerical tasks the exact same way for ten, fifteen, and even twenty years. That seemingly small shift was often enough to turn some people's career perspectives upside down. The new workflows were causing some people to call off work for family, medical, or other leaves of absence on a more frequent basis. And most of these absences didn't even seem to be phony. The new workflows were literally impacting the health of certain staff members. Short-tenured staff was leaving abruptly, and even long-tenured staff seemed to be wavering in commitment.

What was the answer? "We determined that the best way to fix the problem was to get the staff involved with reshaping the way we were shifting to the new workflows." In an environment in which the power must always come from the top (most of what they do is mandate-driven by the state government), they realized that any measure of empowerment they could give to the staff would benefit the organization as a whole. So they tasked employees with leading coaching, training, and guidance through the new processes and systems; they repurposed some longer-tenured employees into new roles that might give them a fresh perspective on the workplace and their role in it; and took a proactive approach to reskilling and reemploying staff rather than cutting them when they failed to meet new mandates.

"We found that leaders had to drive all of this," Urquhart said. "The TalentKeepers engagement survey helped us share data and employee feedback with our managers." That data and feedback opened up new insight for how those managers could improve themselves and their teams. With that knowledge, the organization managed to turn itself from feeling like victims of a state-mandated push toward paperless technology and more like drivers of positive change.

New products. New marketing strategies. New sales goals. New policies. How often do these kinds of changes emerge in your organization? If yours is like just about every other organization on the planet, the answer is "constantly." Almost across the board, the difference between high-performing organizations and everyone else is that the former's leadership structure—from top to bottom—is equipped to foster, manage, and communicate the reasons for that change, details of the change, the benefit of the changes to the organization, and how the change will affect employees. Plus, these organizations let employees know how to get their questions answered as they reflect on what they have learned.

In 2008, TalentKeepers took up a project with a major American communications corporation. Back then the United States was sinking into the depths of the Great Recession— meaning that many organizations were facing a significant decline in business. Meanwhile, because of its exclusive access to a revolutionary piece of technology, this particular organization was growing rapidly. Like any good organization, they still made cuts in response to some of the other parts of their business that were suffering, but for the most part, they prospered during one of the darkest economic periods in history.

Now here's the interesting part about what happens when your frontline employees see this tremendous growth and yet still have to deal with cutbacks. Employees knew the company was making sales hand over fist, and yet suddenly they were losing perks like coffee and chairs in the break room, discretionary spending for managers who wanted to treat their teams to pizza or donuts, and reimbursements for business-related travel or spending.

Understandably, the frontline employees tended to see only the negatives in these kinds of cutbacks. They saw these negatives despite the fact that the reason for the cutting was so the organization wouldn't have to lay anyone off when business inevitably leveled off or began to decline. The organization looked out across the economic landscape and decided that now was the time to be as profitable as possible, because profitability during major recessions is rare.

When viewing the issue from the top-level leadership down, the message was clear: "We're making these tough decisions so our frontline employees have stability in their work." Unfortunately, when we looked at the issue from the front lines up the ladder, what we found was that the message was not being delivered at all. In most cases, what we found was that managers were doing what we earlier called "blaming up." Rather than communicating the desired message about trying to maintain stability, frontline managers were blaming their immediate leaders for the changes. In some cases, those leaders were in turn blaming *their* leaders, and so on and so on all the way to the top.

Blaming Up

"I don't know why they won't let me buy you pizza anymore," a frontline manager would tell an employee who complained about the cutbacks. "And I can tell you one thing for sure: If I were running this store, the last thing I would have cut was the coffee. I mean, how much can coffee possibly cost, anyway?"

Leaders often find themselves caught between a desire to build good relationships with team members and their responsibility to communicate changes and support, defend, or enforce company policies and initiatives. Frequently, leaders have little or no influence in determining the policy, strategy, or decision. What's worse is leaders at many levels often learn of a change in direction or policy at the same time as their team members.

This dynamic occurs with changes in schedules, attendance policies, operational issues, and myriad other topics. Add significant announcements like shifts in strategy, changes in structure or roles, realigned priorities, even mergers and acquisitions, and it's easy to see how leaders can struggle with communicating and defending the steady onrush of changes in today's workplace.

It's a natural human reaction to deflect blame. It's also an all-too-natural response for managers to deflect that blame upward. The true message was that the organization was making cuts because it wanted to be able to keep all its employees in both good times and bad. The message that management was delivering was that they didn't understand the changes and definitely didn't agree with them. When a miscommunication like this occurs, people become distrustful of senior management, resistant to inevitable change, and slow to adopt new processes or procedures.

Think about it from the frontline employee's perspective. If he or she hears from his or her boss, "I don't know what management is thinking," then the message isn't only about disagreement, it's about how "my boss isn't on board about this decision, and in fact, he may be *skeptical* that this is the right decision in the first place." If I'm the frontline employee, what exactly is my incentive to work hard on this new initiative or make the change management is asking me to make? Why should I jump in with both feet if this might not even be the direction we'll be going long term?

Debbie Weaver told us that they have a policy at Stillwater Mining Company: "Don't go down there and ask a guy to do something when you don't know why you're asking them. It's not because 'they told me to.' It's got to be transparent. It's not a secret. Share it and they'll appreciate it. When our leaders understand that notion, it's a big win for our organization."

In all business matters, but particularly during times of change, communication through every level of leadership is incredibly important. The question is, how do we ensure that the right messages are being communicated in the right way to all the right people?

What *Not* to Do

Before we discuss best practices, let's dig in to the all-too-common worst practices we have seen during our years of observation in the field. The top mistake organizational leaders make when approaching a change that has to be passed down through the leadership structure is making the change without including anyone else in the decision. Top leaders send the message down from the executive office and expect everyone to follow it. Obviously that doesn't work. It always leads to confusion from all levels of the organization, and almost always leads to the kind of resistance we mentioned in our opening story about the communications company.

Frequently, organizations attempting to make a change don't give their leadership teams adequate opportunities to be advocates for that change. The leaders don't receive advanced notice about the change; they aren't included in the decision; and they don't receive the kinds of talking points that will help their teams understand how the change will help the organization, benefit all employees in the long run, and why that change is necessary in the first place.

If you are the leader of an organization, one key question to ask is, "Who is telling your frontline employees about you?" The answer is the leader beneath you, the leader beneath her, and the leader beneath him. The leaders beneath you in the leadership structure are the ones who are delivering your message and painting the picture about you. If you feel that the frontline employees and managers are resistant to a change that you have deemed necessary, then you have to ask why they are so resistant. Do they not trust you? How could that be? You're looking out for their best interests, after all.

The issue is simple to identify but sometimes more difficult to resolve. The short answer is that you're doing your half. You're communicating the message you want to communicate. But like the leader who doesn't give any face time to his team, you're not ensuring that the all-important other half gets covered: When you're not there, how are people speaking about you and your message? How would the leaders beneath you describe you? Do they value you? Do they understand you? Do they understand why you want to make this change?

Such a shortfall in communication can devastate any number of organizational initiatives. The message about how and why a change occurs so often gets muddled, misunderstood, and resisted because *people* are doing the communicating. Unless we as leaders recognize the value in each individual person and appreciate that value by tailoring the message to the individual who must receive it, then we will not maximize the value of any important change.

We know that everyone comes from a different background: different upbringings, generational factors, and matters of individual values. Every individual values something different about her job. We all come to work for a different reason. If we hope to communicate the right message about change, then we need to know what those reasons and values are and make the message personal.

Let's imagine a scenario where you have to announce cutbacks to your organization's benefit packages. If the message is simply, "We need to make cuts so we can remain profitable and all of you can keep your jobs," that message might seem benevolent on its surface, but it doesn't play the same to everyone. For some people, job stability is the key motivating factor about their work. For others, stability isn't nearly as important as keeping those benefits they have come to enjoy.

The message has to be tailor-made for each individual. "Susan, I know you're here because you need the benefits because you have a sick child" is one kind of message. "Richard, I know you're here because the schedule works for you right now as you're in school getting your degree" is another. "Christine, I understand that you're here because you want to climb the corporate ladder" is yet another. Each of these three people has a different motivation about work, and each of these three people will need to hear a different version of that same core message about cutting benefits to not have to cut anyone's job. Recognizing the individual's specific needs allows the leader to be better at shaping the experience of the change to meet specific goals.

Here's an interesting question: With messages about organizational change, does the message get clearer and more accurate the closer you get to the top of the organization? The short answer, at least for most organizations, is yes. We find, in fact, that in most cases the closer each level of management is to the top, the more engaged it is, not only with communicating messages, but with all aspects of leadership. We've found two reasons for this. First, people who are higher up the ladder of leadership tend to be more committed to their roles because they have been with an organization longer and have more responsibility. With a longer tenure comes more experience to deliver the correct message to a team and to react to change with a level head. This person has seen more revolutions of the business cycle than most, after all. They've seen the impact of different policies and procedures over time. This leader is more stable and less swayed by the smaller things that might sway newer leaders and employees.

"Historically, we have been a top-down, hierarchical organization," Steve Urquhart said about the Clerk of Courts in Orange County. "But through our Leadership Academy Development Program, we are working to instill that sense of ownership to the middle-management level." They are doing this by setting clearer standards and holding everyone accountable to meeting those standards, providing nearly real-time feedback on performance metrics and qualitative coaching, celebrating successes and creating a strong sense of team identity, and using feedback to advocate and champion for improvement on all levels.

"One of the most powerful things we do is bring best practices from the industry back to the team," Steve said. The strategy has worked in spades. The Orange County Clerk's call center had a reputation for being the place where employees were sent if they were underperforming in another division. But recently, thanks in part to their decision to empower middle managers, that call center returned some of the highest engagement scores in the organization. "It's all because of that one manager," Steve suggested. "He addressed that idea that this call center was kind of known as the place of last resort. He made sure that it was clear that the call center and the role it played was of significant value to the organization. It is the front lines for almost all customer interaction. He really turned around their perception of themselves."

That manager listened actively to his team, took their feedback to heart, and held his own supervisor to the high standard he held himself. "He pushes his employees," Steve explained, "but also makes sure to validate and value them and show them that their feedback is being heard. He actively works to improve issues for his employees."

The turnaround at that one call center has been incredible. Now other managers are starting to pay attention. "This call center was once the lowest of lows, and now it's a cohesive team that's valued and respected in the organization." Other managers and teams have started to adopt the strategies that have been so effective.

The second reason higher-level leaders are more engaged is the higher up you go on the ladder, the more talented the leader tends to be—not only with performing their roles, but with *leading* people.

That high-level leader didn't get into that position by being merely adequate at the job and at leading teams. She was promoted (at least in theory) because she was good at leading people.

The LEI numbers we have gathered over the years bear this out. Picture a staircase of LEI scores as you get higher in an organization. More often than not, that staircase leads upward, and the higher you go, the higher the score.

There are exceptions to this rule, however. Sometimes we see an inversion in the stairs, where one leadership level is less engaged than the one beneath it. This can be a big problem, because it's more difficult for a team to be engaged if its boss is not. The leader is the lens through which that team views everything, and if that lens is muddied with a low LEI score, then they're not seeing the correct message. If left unchecked, it will decrease the level of engagement beneath that underperforming manager and, in fact, will continue rolling downhill to the front lines.

It All Rolls Downhill

Sometimes an organization makes the mistake of focusing only on frontline employees. They will put tons of resources into that frontline employee level. They will offer training and learning opportunities, spectacular incentives, and plenty of chances to advance. When this happens, the leadership teams that manage that frontline group sometimes feel left out, underappreciated, and as if there are no programs for them to take advantage of.

Here's an intriguing relationship we have observed: Your frontline employee engagement will rarely be higher than your frontline leader engagement. Why? The reason is that those leaders are usually the glue that can keep those frontline employees with the organization. That's a key metric that we evaluate: the engagement and retention levels of that frontline leadership group.

Other times, we will find entire leadership teams that show lower LEI scores, which can make it difficult to break out of the circle. Imagine a frontline leader and the manager she reports to both having low scores. In this situation, we have the junior manager taking the lead from the senior manager, and the two of them feed into patterns of behaviors and opinions that can be damaging to the whole team or teams that serve under them. Over time, they can both get off track on what's valuable and working for engagement.

People hear what their leaders tell them, but far more importantly, they *know* what they see their leaders do. Frontline employees tend to mimic their leaders' behaviors in their own style, making it difficult to break that pattern. When we find pairs or teams of leaders with low scores, we always work to compel senior leadership above that pair or team to get involved, because their influence is key to change.

What to Do: Sharing Down

Your greatest ally to reverse blaming up and strengthening your culture is increased communication. This is what we call "sharing down." In any culture, communication is the lubricant for effecting change, and silence is the friction.

We know that the problems we see on this front are similar from organization to organization and leader to leader. We also know that the ways to attack these problems are virtually the same. First, whenever possible, providing advance notice to all levels of leadership about an upcoming announcement, policy change, new goal, and so on is important. This gives them time to personally react to the change before they think about how their teams will react. Sometimes those initial reactions can be negative. It's important to give leaders time to stew through that negative reaction and come to embrace the positive business need for this change before they communicate it to their teams.

Second, management must give leaders the right talking points to share about the reasons for this decision. It's not enough to say, "We have to make this change" to survive, thrive, or whatever the message happens to be. Your leaders must know the business drivers that you're hoping to influence with this decision. They need to know what alternative strategies management considered before arriving at this decision. And they need to know every element of why this decision will benefit the organization. Then—and we can't stress this highly enough—leaders must use these talking points when they address their teams.

The third tactic is to give leaders an upward feedback channel to go to with questions from their team that they can't answer. This lets them quickly get an answer and provide it to their team, which builds confidence for the team, confidence for the leader, and confidence between the team and their leader. Rather than reacting in a way that says, "I don't know why management is doing this" in a negative tone, now every leader feels as though he or she is empowered to get answers. Meanwhile, the team also sees the leader as someone who can get answers, which builds trust in that individual leader from that team. Now when a team member has a question, he or she is going to go to that manager because that manager has consistently been able to get answers to questions he has had. As an added (and highly powerful) bonus, this upward feedback channel helps inform *you* how the delivery of your message about change is going.

There's a litmus test in all of this. If you want to know whether your message is being delivered appropriately, listen to your managers as they describe changes. Listen specifically for two words: If the leaders are saying, "*They* want us to do this," then they aren't engaged with the message. They're blaming up. If they say, "*We* want to do this," then they're owning and advocating the decision. They're "sharing down."

This difference allows leaders to bridge gaps, strengthen the bond of their teams, and always ensure that the message is well received. With these tighter bonds and stronger messages, leaders at all levels take the next step toward that higher LEI score. This brings them closer to being able to have those difficult conversations about career.

5 Solving the Career Growth Dilemma

Career issues remain the top reason that employees are voluntarily leaving their jobs in the United States. This trend has happened seven years in a row based on our national research. And it's not always about upward mobility or a lack thereof. It's about growth—growing skills and knowledge, gaining responsibility for roles and tasks, being exposed to things that make one better at one's job, and so on. No matter what organization we're talking about, employees care a great deal about these matters, particularly millennials. Because they care so much about these matters, having conversations between leaders and employees is critical, and yet these conversations are not happening as frequently as they should be.

If an employee leaves in the first year, it's most likely because they had missed expectations or were a poor fit based on the skills required. The next biggest reason is a lack of advancement opportunities. Figure 5.1 plots the biggest reasons employees voluntarily leave their jobs within the first twelve months on the job, excluding pay. We always exclude pay when asking these sorts of questions because everyone, even you, has a number—an amount of money for which

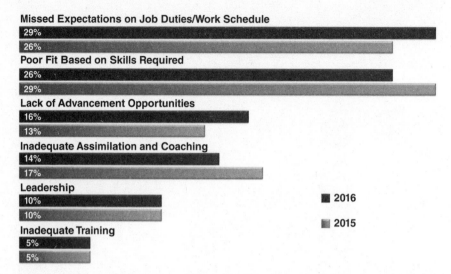

Figure 5.1   Reasons that employees voluntarily leave their jobs in the first year.

you would leave your current job. Fortunately, even the allure of more money can be moderated by engagement. Research shows that if an employee is engaged, it will take at least 20% more pay to get them to leave simply for a higher salary. Conversely, if an employee is not engaged, they will leave for as little as 5% more, or even less.

Employees who leave after their first twelve months on the job do so for varying reasons. Nearly half of all the reasons to leave for these employees are career driven, with "upward advancement" accounting for 30% of all reasons, followed by "lack of growth experiences within current role" at 19%. Figure 5.2 depicts the reasons employees leave after their first year on the job, excluding pay.

Clearly, career plays a central role in the "leave decisions" for low- and longer-tenured employees. The best person to have these conversations about career growth is the frontline leader. Unfortunately, not enough of them engage in these conversations, and for good reasons: First, some frontline leaders don't think it's their job to have these conversations (and why would they, since their bosses didn't have

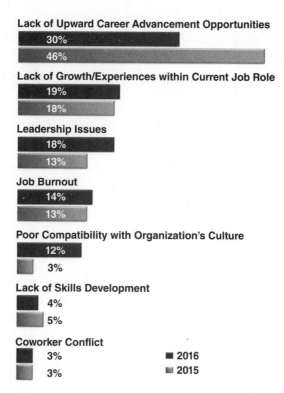

Lack of Upward Career Advancement Opportunities
30%
46%

Lack of Growth/Experiences within Current Job Role
19%
18%

Leadership Issues
18%
13%

Job Burnout
14%
13%

Poor Compatibility with Organization's Culture
12%
3%

Lack of Skills Development
4%
5%

Coworker Conflict
3%   ■ 2016
3%   ▨ 2015

Figure 5.2 Reasons that employees voluntarily leave their jobs after the first year.

these conversations with them?); second, they don't want to make a mistake like promising somebody a raise or a promotion and then not being able to deliver later (this compels them to think that it's better not to talk about career goals at all); third, it's so much easier to tell an employee what she wants to hear rather than the truth.

That last point is huge, and we see it often. We see leaders telling an employee that she is doing a great job and is on "the list" of people in line for a promotion, then turning around and telling *their* leaders that this same employee is nowhere near ready for a promotion. Leadership takes honesty, which requires greater skill. It's hard to tell people things they don't want to hear, but the best leaders do so in a constructive, positive, and career-affirming way.

Recognize the Right Way

Everybody loves to be praised, right? Sure, but not everybody loves to be praised in exactly the same way. Just because Marissa really enjoyed that glowing speech you gave about her in front of everyone in the office doesn't mean Jerome will too. Praise is a valuable component to the manager/employee relationship, but only if that praise is personal. This means that the best leaders make the message unique to what each individual values most.

You don't want to attempt to do something good by recognizing someone publically if they would prefer private recognition (that's one great way to turn a positive into a negative). If this person would love to have an email that she can read over and over again, then don't miss that opportunity by simply praising her face-to-face. The flip side is also true. Some people much prefer face-to-face recognition—and that includes millennials, believe it or not. Some like to be treated to lunch. Others would appreciate a handwritten note.

Bertha Johnson highlighted what they are doing at the city of Durham to determine individual preferences for each employee. Their E-3 (Employee Engagement Exercise) Program assists supervisors with employee engagement by helping them learn how they like to be recognized for their successes. The program also helps bring to light the strength and skills that each employee likes to use on the job, and what areas they would like to focus on in developing their talents. "Developing a partnership involves each party recognizing the other's contributions, strengths, and preferences," Johnson said.

Here's another example: While we were working with that same communications company, we found that the market with the highest engagement scores and business metrics (both sales and service) got there in part because of one tremendous action one of the vice presidents (VP) was doing. The highest-level leader in this market was sending handwritten notes to frontline employees who had achieved certain criteria or met specific goals. Over the course of three months, that VP had sent over two hundred of these notes. These notes became highly valued in the market of 1,500 employees. Now we're talking about 15 to 20% of the people working in this market had received a handwritten note of congratulations and praise.

And here's the really powerful part: Most of the recipients didn't take these notes home or stash them away in their desks. Instead, they would put them up on the bulletin board in the back of the store. This allowed them to show how proud they were to have been recognized, which in turn raised morale considerably. It got to the point where people would clamor to see who would be the one to go get the mail that day in the hopes of finding another letter from the VP.

Imagine the value of this action. How much does it cost to write a note? It costs nothing. In fact, recognizing an employee for a job well done *never* has to cost a dime. Recognition is free, but it goes a long, long way.

Trust Each Other with Your Careers

Early in TalentKeepers' history, we received a couple of emails from someone claiming to be with the CIA. This person said he wanted to hire us to help with engagement and retention within the agency. We deleted the emails, figuring they were a prank by some colleague looking to make us laugh. But then we got a call. "Really," the caller said, "I'm with the CIA. Please don't hang up on me."

Still sort of in disbelief, we listened as the contact explained that his organization was struggling with retaining agents.

"I'm not sure we can help you," we said. "We work with retailers, call centers, and other professional environments. We deal with trust, communication, coaching, and career issues."

"Those are the exact reasons people leave the CIA," the contact insisted. "In the field, we trust each other with our lives, but when we return to the office, we don't trust each other with our careers."

We agreed to work with them.

As we transition into this chapter and delve deeper into the subject of career conversations, keep in mind that the higher you rise up the leadership ladder, the harder it is to have these career discussions. After all, the higher you climb, the fewer the opportunities you have to advance. Intraleadership dynamics become more acute when the people doing the talking are more competitive. In some ways, it's easier to trust someone with your life than it is to trust them with your career.

Shifting Career Aspirations

Picture yourself as a frontline employee in your organization. Let's imagine that you've been in your role for three years. During that time, you have gotten to know, respect, and enjoy the company of your immediate supervisor. He is a great boss. He always speaks to you about what you need and expect to receive from your job. He coaches you and helps you evolve into a genuinely spectacular contributor to your team. Because the two of you have had so many conversations over the years, you feel confident that he knows your aspirations to be promoted into a leadership role—and in fact, that you aspire to rise to the director's chair one day. You enjoy coming to work in part because you like working for your supervisor, and also because you feel confident you have a future here.

Now let's imagine that this supervisor of yours has just announced that he will be leaving his position for a promotion in another department—or worse, maybe he's leaving the organization altogether. Now, that amazing person to work for and that great advocate for your future with the organization is gone. His replacement is someone you've never even seen before, let alone met or with whom you've had the chance to work. What's your first concern? Well, your first concern might be about all the subtle changes that might add up to a big difference in your day-to-day routine. The new boss is likely to have her own way of doing things and her own set of expectations, so what is that going to mean for you? That's scary enough, and in fact, for some people, it's sometimes plenty of impetus to start looking for another job. The mutual trust and commitment you shared is walking out the door.

You, though, are invested in this organization and can still envision yourself working here ten years from now. So what's your next thought? Probably you're worried that all those conversations you had with your former supervisor—concerning your expectations, your goals, your needs—have just gone out the door with him. Now you'll have to start over with this new person and hope that she gets you, respects you, and wants to help you as much as your former supervisor. Will your new leader share the same commitment to your growth and aspirations as your old boss? That might seem like a long shot. After all, your former supervisor was your favorite boss ever, and in no small part thanks to his uncommon willingness to listen, bond, and do what he needed to do to make you feel valued and on track for that promotion.

These are the effects of an organizational change, and as we discussed in the previous chapter, change—both organizational and personal—can lead to an erosion of engagement. Your commitment to your job and the company remains strong, but your productivity may suffer in the coming days, weeks, or even months in part because now you're thinking about how, at best, you'll have to go in to talk to your new supervisor and regurgitate all that information that your former supervisor already knew. Then you also have to hope that this new supervisor will agree with you that your goals are important and that you're capable of meeting those you set.

But imagine how the conversation—and indeed, your impression of your new supervisor—changes if that new supervisor comes to *you* and says, "So I was just reading these notes on your goals, needs, and aspirations with the organization. This is all really great. I was just wondering if you could update me on what's left to do here? Where do you feel like you are in this timeline you've set? What kind of progress have you made? How do you see that you've changed in your role and improved the team? What do I need to do to take you to that next level?"

That's a totally different and an entirely powerful conversation. As a frontline employee, now you're realizing that your new supervisor is taking the time to learn about you and show you she cares. You understand that, like your old boss, this new boss isn't going to treat you like a number. She's going to treat you like a person who has values and is valued. It takes the conversation from, "So, tell me everything I need to know about you and what you do here," to "Tell me what's important to you right now so I can help you get it." A leader who is equipped to say something like this—especially if that leader is then skilled enough to shut up and listen to the answers—has nearly everything she needs to solve the career dilemma. It doesn't matter whether you're speaking with a boomer or a gen Xer or a millennial; *everyone* appreciates this kind of conversation, and that appreciation goes a long way toward improving engagement.

The Stay Interview

You've heard of exit interviews. You've probably even conducted or sat in on a few. Their value to any organization is tremendous, because here we have an opportunity to learn from a departing employee all those factors that are causing him to leave. This allows us to assess how we might make changes to prevent similar departures from happening in the future. This data is incredibly useful, which is exactly why such a high percentage of organizations employ the strategy.

What would make this kind of data even more useful would be if your organization gathered it *throughout* every employee's career life cycle. Many organizations get a part of the way there by implementing selection and onboarding programs that include some form of assessment or evaluation that can be used to learn more about the new employee's potential for growth. They may ask the right questions about each incoming employee's goals, needs, and expectations. Unfortunately, too many of these organizations then stick that information in a drawer and never revisit it—at least not until it's time to conduct the exit interview. So what about all the in-betweens? If we look at the time between when an employee starts and when an employee leaves, are we thinking that the employee's goals, needs, and expectations don't matter anymore? Or are we under the impression that they never change?

Of course they change. These factors are in flux throughout the career life cycle, right along with the knowledge, skill, and engagement of each employee. This is why we advocate for organizations to collect the appropriate data early and often, keep this data with the employee, and revisit it as often as possible.

One key to attacking the career dilemma is to use a systemic approach. Start by gathering information from each employee, and building on this data with each subsequent (ideally monthly or at least quarterly) conversation between leader and employee. If you talk to the people you count on frequently, you have a much better understanding of who they are, what they expect, what they need, and what it will take to compel them to stay with your organization. That information is so much more valuable and actionable than the exit interview data related to why that employee left you.

Conducting these stay interviews on a regular basis through a short questionnaire also allows the organization to aggregate the data, which opens leaderships' eyes to what their employees want at any given time during their tenure. New hires from one generation tend to value and want different things than longer-tenured employees from other generations. People occupying one role within an organization often share preferences that differ from people occupying another. Knowing these differences and having this key data at hand allows leadership to take action and ensure that everyone is having their expectations met. If trust is the most important point across the board, for example, then how have you engendered trust between leaders and their teams? Stay interviews allow you to audit your own career offerings and see how they fit with your team's needs.

Stay interviews are well worth the effort. Figure 5.3 shows the financial benefit one of our clients realized by using stay interviews to increase retention. These types of positive returns are almost always achievable when stay interviews are properly implemented.

The stay interview strategy also helps solve the dilemma we presented at the opening of the chapter. If this data follows the employee, then even a leadership change can be seamless in terms of its effect on engagement. The stay interview data allows the new leader to discuss with each team member everything that has already been documented, reference that documentation in the future, and always know how to make sure the leader is meeting the needs of each employee.

Good survey data—whether gathered anonymously as with most engagement surveys or nonanonymously as with a stay interview survey—can provide valuable information for an organization. A

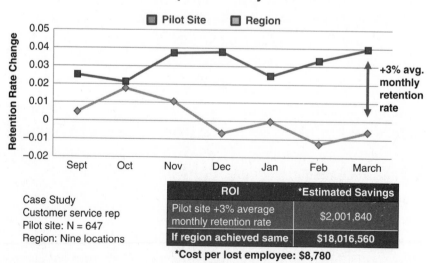

Figure 5.3 The financial benefit a client realized by using stay interviews to increase retention.

major hotel chain recently presented an anonymous survey to all of its employees in a certain category of its business. The responses they received from these employees were surprising at times, but always valuable. They learned the more surface-level data like the notion that they were losing 48% of new hires in less than six months while retaining only 6% for more than five years. It seemed that most employees who left did so for personal reasons, but job abandonment, new job opportunities, and a failure to meet job expectations or company policy rounded out the top five. You know what reason was at the very bottom? "Dissatisfied with pay." For some in the organization's leadership structure, that came as a huge shock, as the impression had always been that attracting better talent meant paying better wages. Across the board, this is simply not so. Pay is important, but it only goes so far.

The truth was that most respondents, regardless of background, were far more interested in questions about how they would get recognized in front of the team, whether rumors about changes in workflow or leadership were true, and how they might move up the ranks with a promotion. Many respondents who admitted to lower levels of engagement suggested that they wanted more variety in their work and wished they felt more challenged. These factors mattered a great deal to nearly everyone who took part in the surveys. It's no surprise that they all have to do with the quality of leadership.

What Causes People to Stay?

What do you think employees prefer most in a leader? The top preference is trust. Frontline employees in every organization we have ever worked with want to feel like they can trust their

(continued)

What Causes People to Stay? (cont'd)

leaders and that their leaders work to build trust within the teams. Then comes the matter of communication, followed by retention, followed by development and coaching. People feel more secure in their careers and valued at work if they report to a leader they can trust, someone who is open and honest with them, someone who understands what it takes to keep them happy and productive, and someone who offers them opportunities to improve their knowledge/abilities and expand their roles.

You know what else is interesting about that hotel chain's surveys? With all the preaching we've been doing about the different preferences between different generations, when it comes to preferences about leadership qualities, *it did not matter* whether the respondent was a boomer, gen Xer, or millennial. Everyone valued trust, communication, retention, and talent development in at least their top five. The same was true regardless of tenure. Whether you've been with the organization for less than six months or more than five years, trust remains squarely at the top of your list. Communication sticks around in the top three, while retention and talent development stay in the top four. This organization employs people who work on-site and from home, and the survey also revealed that the environment mattered little either. Whether on-site or off, respondents overwhelmingly favored trust, communication, retention, and talent development.

When it came to career preferences, the organization learned that maintaining a work-life balance trumped even the opportunity to increase or maintain compensation based on contributions. Having fulfilling work to do rated nearly as high as compensation, as well. Professional growth and new opportunities also checked in as key values. The interesting part? When it comes to career preferences, tenure and generation *do* matter. For the employee who has been around for less than six months, career opportunities top the charts. That's only natural, of course. When you're first starting with a new job, your main concern is how you can advance your career. In years one through three, financial worth rates as the highest factor. This should come as no surprise, either, given that people tend to focus on making money as they establish themselves in a new role. And what do people who have been around longer than five years value the most? Well-being. If you've been with an organization for a long time, your primary concern shifts to work-life balance. By now you're comfortable in your role and with your compensation. Now you just want to find a way to feel rewarded and enjoy your work while still having plenty of time and energy for your family. Figure 5.4 shows how career preferences varied by tenure in one client organization. Expect these variances in yours, too.

Interestingly, work-life balance was ranked highest for gen Xers and baby boomers, but it came in third for millennials, the generation with whom many people have associated a focus on work-life balance. For millennials, compensation was the highest rated factor, followed by career opportunities and then well-being. For boomers, the preferences were practically reversed, with career opportunities ranking at the bottom.

What can a leader do to ensure that every employee feels as if their needs are understood and being met? Regular stay interviews go a long way, but as we mentioned in the previous chapter, you also have to know how each individual values engagement and recognition interactions with their leaders.

(continued)

What Causes People to Stay? (cont'd)

		1–6 Months	1–3 Years	5+ Years
	1	Career Opportunities	Financial Worth	Well-Being
	2	Well-Being	Well-Being	Financial Worth
	3	Professional Growth	Professional Growth	Work Fulfillment
	4	Financial Worth	Work Fulfillment	Professional Growth
	5	Work Fulfillment	Career Opportunities	Stability
	6	New Experiences	New Experiences	New Experiences
	7	Stability	Stability	Career Opportunities

Most Important ↑

Figure 5.4 Variation in career preference by tenure.

Do they prefer in person, email, a phone call, recognition in front of the whole team, lunch, a handwritten letter?

By a wide margin, respondents in the hotel chain's survey, and every survey of the sort that we have ever conducted, ranked in person the highest for both engagement preferences and recognition preferences. Faceless modes of communication like email and phone calls scaled farther down the list, with team announcements trailing behind. It might surprise you to learn that, out of all respondents, millennials were the ones most likely to value in-person meetings about engagement and recognition. Millennials are supposed to be the ones constantly glued to their phones and living in a world of social media communication. Even so, they preferred in-person engagement meetings at a 67% rate versus gen Xers and boomers, who preferred them at 49% and 50%, respectively.

Tenure matters little regarding communication preference. No matter how long the employee has been with the organization, she tends to prefer in-person meetings. They value it highest when they have been in their roles for less than six months, but it remains the top preference throughout an employee's time with the organization.

"The bottom line is that the leader should believe in employee engagement," said Donna Fayko of North Carolina's Rowan County. "It is important to understand how critical it is to create a work-life balance for staff. You also should keep in touch with the ways you motivate the different generations that you're hiring. Some millennials are so energized that they believe they can start on day one as a frontline worker and become the director by the next day. When expectations are so high, you have to find creative ways to keep them engaged."

In Donna's view, communication and knowledge are power. "Open communication between all levels of leadership in your organization is the ultimate goal. Not all decisions should be made at the top. The opening of communication and the sharing of power creates better partnership and collaboration."

More than anything, making people want to stay is a matter of (1) keeping it fun, and (2) giving them opportunities to advance. At Rowan County, employees dress up for Halloween, hold an annual Super Bowl party, regularly sponsor games and friendly competitions, and so on. They also believe in standardized supervision and coaching, training newcomers toward success, and demonstrating opportunities for upward mobility by way of lead-worker routines and other informal leadership opportunities for frontline workers hoping to advance. "The idea is to avoid people getting stagnant in their roles," Donna advises. "Anytime you can give staff an opportunity for growth, it will benefit you."

Career Growth and Accountability

We know what needs to happen if we hope to engage and retain more talent: Leaders have to conduct these stay interviews regularly with every employee, and ideally, they need to do it in person. It all seems pretty cut and dried, so why aren't these kinds of career conversations happening more often (if at all) and in more organizations?

The surface reason is simple: Most leaders don't know who's responsible for having these conversations. Some think this is the role of human resources. Some think it should fall to the frontline leaders. Others believe it should be senior management's responsibility. Well, let's resolve this issue right here and now: These conversations need to be happening between frontline leaders and frontline employees.

Clarity about who is responsible for these conversations is critical. Absent clear roles and accountability for having these conversations, your leaders and employees will flounder, and too few employees will have a career-growth conversation, which greatly increases the chances they'll become disengaged and leave. We have developed a model to depict what should be considered for career growth and who should be accountable for it. We call it the Career Growth and Accountability Model, which is shown in Figure 5.5.

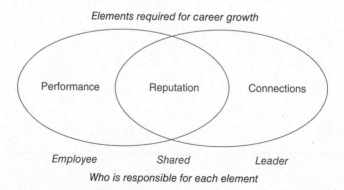

Figure 5.5 The Career Growth and Accountability Model.

We must address three key factors, and we will do so in depth in a moment, but first, keep in mind the big picture: As leaders, the perception we're striving for is that we're trustworthy, honest, and open in our communication and our presentation of opportunities to each employee. The perception needs to be that the way you get promoted at this organization is transparent and objective. Every employee must believe that if he works hard and does what's valued here, the sky is the limit. No one has to do any sucking up or jockeying to get on the "good list." It's all about effort and results. This perception eliminates favoritism, ensures that everybody remains in the loop on what is expected of them, and keeps your best talent with you.

Performance

A prerequisite to getting career growth opportunities is to perform well in your current role. The employee is primarily accountable for her own performance. The leader is responsible for setting performance expectations, providing feedback on how the employee is performing, and giving appropriate coaching to help the employee meet the expectations. Highly effective leaders understand that it is their job to train every employee to reach performance goals and that level of competence necessary to taking on new responsibilities and even new positions in the organization. However, at the end of the day, the employee has to perform. Each employee must understand that her current job is the springboard to any other job in the organization. If she is underperforming in her current job, the probability of advancement goes way down. The accountability for performance falls squarely on the employee.

Reputation

Reputation includes everything from your work ethic, your dress, your willingness to volunteer, your willingness to go above and beyond, how well you get along with others, and so on. You need the right reputation if you're going to advance. At first glance, this might seem obvious, but many people, regardless of tenure or background, are often unaware of what a key role reputation plays.

A leader needs to be honest with employees before they will begin to understand the importance of reputation. Likewise, the employee will have to embrace the notion. These two things can't happen if the leader isn't conducting regular discussions on performance and career aspirations with the team member. After all, how can the leader know for certain what is causing these reputation issues if she doesn't ask? If you have an employee who never stays one minute past 5 p.m., the surface assumption might be that this employee is lazy, not dedicated, or hates this job so much that he can't wait to get home at the end of the day. But what if the truth is something much deeper than that? What if that employee has no choice but to leave immediately because he has to pick up a child from daycare no later than 5:30? Then, the perspective changes. Additionally, team members may have some blind spots regarding certain elements of their reputation. Therefore, the accountability for reputation is on both the leader and the employee.

Connections

The connections factor has two elements. The first is this: As a leader, I want to connect this person who wants advancement to other people in the organization who may be able to offer that individual opportunities for career growth. I need to be talking up my talent. When I hear about another leader who needs help with something that I feel would be a great fit for a talented employee, I need to express what a great candidate she would be for the role.

The second element is that I must allow my team member to learn more about other areas, responsibilities, or roles in the organization that may interest him. For example, I might arrange for him to have coffee with another supervisor from another function so he can learn more about what that function does. Then the employee can make an informed decision about whether this will fit his needs. The accountability for making these connections falls largely to the leader.

The greatest value of the Career Growth and Accountability model is that it clarifies roles and responsibilities for career growth, and thereby helps to address some common misunderstandings that cause so many leaders to hesitate when discussing career issues with team members. Once again, this is the clearest path to a more engaged and talented workforce.

Job Stratification

Since career growth is such a powerful engagement and retention factor, we developed a tactic to provide more opportunities for career growth called "job stratification." This structural tactic opens up more levels of opportunity to grow employees into skills, experiences, and eventually, roles. Rather than having just two levels of employment— leader and frontline employee—many organizations create new titles and responsibilities that set teams up with more frequent steps toward the top. Some organizations call these roles things like "Team Leader 1, 2, and 3," and others go with the more traditional "assistant supervisor," "associate supervisor," "senior supervisor," and so on. The idea is that designating more roles with different titles and increasing responsibility not only gives the employee the sense of more room for advancement in shorter order (something that plays especially well with millennials), it also helps better prepare each employee for that ultimate leadership role, as they can learn pieces of that particular job in small doses over a longer period.

WOWs, Wet Socks, and Snorkels

We have already seen how employees from different generations or tenures will value at least slightly different things. However, we also know that different employees perform at different levels, and as such, they must be managed differently. You can't manage your most talented employee in the same way as your employee with the lowest performance levels. The great leader must tailor the message and the management style to the skill of the employee and to their position on the career spectrum.

In our research, we have found that one particularly effective tool for leaders to use is to categorize each member of the team into one of three performance groups. This exercise is valuable enough on its own, but the best practice is to then have each team member assign themselves into one of the three groups as well. This helps both leader and team member understand where perceptions of performance might be differing. Having these clean and clearly identifiable categories helps open up the communication and get everyone on board with where they stand and what they need to do to advance.

What are the categories? As the title to this section suggests, they are "WOW," "Wet Socks," and "Snorkels." The acronym "WOW" stands for "Walks on Water." The employees who fall into this category are your absolute top performers. "Wet Socks" are your second-tier performers, so named because they often walk on water, but occasionally stumble and get their socks wet. Tier three are your Snorkels, who get their names because they operating somewhere below the performance line—or in other words, they're usually underwater on their work, and need a snorkel to breathe.

It doesn't matter what kind of team you lead and what kind of organization you work for; you have at least one person on your team that fits into each of these three categories. The goal, then, is to get the snorkels above water, coach the wet socks to be WOWs, and create an environment where WOWs flourish.

Of course, you need three different approaches to manage the employees in each category. You can't interact with and coach a WOW in the same way you do a snorkel. The first step is knowing the qualities of the people with whom you're dealing.

WOWs

WOWs are really good at what they do. They're creative. They think through things that even you as a leader might not have considered. A good leader surrounds himself with WOWs, even if those WOWs are better and more talented than he is.

When you give a WOW an assignment, the best way to describe that assignment is to focus on the outcomes. "Here's what we need. Here's what success looks like in this project." The best leaders will tell their WOWs every possible angle to success on a given task or project, but they never tell them *how* to get there. For a WOW, if you tell them the how, you remove the opportunity for them to wow you with their solutions (pun very much intended). WOWs often find solutions that go above and beyond what you as the leader might envision on your own.

Now, of course, we aren't all comfortable with handing things off to someone else and hoping their strategies deliver. To mitigate risk, you can ask a WOW to go and think about what they would do to achieve the results you're looking for before they come back and present their strategy to you. This gives you an opportunity to adjust that plan to make sure it's feasible and appropriate. If that sounds like macromanaging, that's because it is. Macromanaging is the only way to effectively manage a WOW.

Wet Socks

Wet Socks are an intriguing group because they have shown flashes of potential to reach that WOW level. The first thing to ask a Wet Sock is whether they're willing to put in whatever effort necessary to become a WOW. Not everyone answers in the same way. They might be a Wet Sock because they don't aspire to reach that next level. Or it could be that they weren't aware that they weren't already on that next level. Or maybe they have an extra issue at home, like an aging parent or a sick child, which prevents them from putting in the extra time that may be required to become a WOW. Whatever the case, the message needs to be, "I think you can excel in your role and be great, but it's going to take some work. Are you interested?"

If they say yes, the next question is, "Are you aware of what is preventing you from being a WOW?" Most people don't see these dynamics intuitively. Self-reflection is difficult to manage. Most people have a blind spot regarding the factors that are preventing them from being great.

Once you have been open and honest with each other about where the employee stands and needs to improve, the conversation can shift toward discussing what the worker can do to overcome current issues, improve themselves, and reach that next level. Once you discuss mutually agreed-upon performance goals and timeframes for achieving them, you have an effective start to moving a Wet Sock to a WOW!

Snorkels

With Snorkels, micromanagement becomes necessary. You need to get granular on what is preventing them from achieving at least an acceptable level of performance. For example, imagine a salesperson consistently misses their quota. In this case, you need to start talking about the basics. "How many interactions are you having with potential customers every day?" If that number is too low, then you know that the employee has no hope of ever reaching the goal, and increasing the number of prospects the employee speaks with daily is a good place to start. On the other hand, if it's the right number, then the conversations shifts to what exactly it is that this employee is saying to the customer. For Snorkels, ask questions such as, "How well do you understand the product? How are you addressing the customer's concerns? How is the conversation going?"

The best practice in this case is to observe the Snorkel's behavior in the field. Give input and suggest specific behaviors that need coaching. Do this daily. Micromanage. Based on the answers you receive, you will learn whether this person is capable of learning and advancing.

No matter which level of employee you're speaking with, always remember to be honest. If they're going to improve, they need to know clearly where they stand, even if that conversation is difficult. Once you have had that open and honest communication with your employees, asking your leader to rate those same employees is often a positive step. This helps you see the picture more objectively. If there isn't agreement—whether between you and your employees or you and your leader—then you know you have work to do. If your Snorkel thinks they're a WOW, they're going to resist coaching, because they think they're already great. In cases like these, you will need to invest more time and effort into delivering the message and helping the employee rise.

As a final point, don't wait on this. The longer you wait, the longer it will take you to determine whether your Snorkels will advance. You will also have employees spending more time in a role that isn't suited to them. Maybe this person is a Snorkel because she is not in a job that fits her purview. Maybe she would be more valuable elsewhere in the organization.

The greater damage by not acting now is that if you do not address Snorkels, you stand the chance of losing WOWs and Wet Socks to other organizations. Winners, after all, want to work for winning teams. In this way, Snorkels have more impact than on their own performance. Their poor performance could drive down morale and even compel high performers to leave.

In closing, remember that leaders need to embrace career conversations with employees. Focus the discussion on what drives the employee at work, where she is on the performance continuum, and what steps will help keep her engaged. This is *leadership*, not management.

6 New Rules for Building a Leadership Team

A few years ago, we were working with a client who was running a large call center in Charlotte, North Carolina. At that center was a manager named Leon. When we first started working with this client, Leon was the manager of a day shift. His employees regarded him highly, and his team performed exceedingly well on all measures. Then something changed for him—there's that old, reliable *change* coming back again. Leon decided that he wanted to go back to school to get a degree, and the only way to do that would be to switch to an evening shift so he would have enough time during the day to attend his classes.

Now, completely switching a work schedule is a big, often uncomfortable change for most people, to say nothing of switching teams. Not many people would volunteer to make such a dramatic change. But when Leon announced his decision to move to an evening shift, nine of his fifteen team members *went with him*. That's nine people who valued Leon's spectacular leadership to the point where they were willing to literally turn their working lives upside down just to stay with him.

Obviously, Leon scored quite highly on the Leader Engagement Index. He is the perfect example of how responsibility and accountability for retaining talent needs to move out from the HR department and into the front lines. As we have discussed, competitive pay, benefits, and team-building programs, while helpful, are no longer enough to keep workers from shopping for their next opportunity. Leaders like Leon are an organization's best defense against unwanted turnover and keeping valued talent longer.

But how prepared are leaders to perform this critical role? Getting leaders to accept accountability and learn new retention and engagement skills may first take some unlearning. Those fundamental assumptions about the availability and skill of the workforce may get in the way. A couple of assumptions are that you need to hire only the highest quality people, and you need to ensure that you always put the right people in the right jobs. But what should a leader do when there aren't enough "highest-quality" people with all of the right skills to go around?

Many terrific leadership formulas discuss charisma, focus, passion, and courage—and thousands more cover good, solid management skills—but what if you're losing 50 percent or more of your employees a year, like some organizations already are? Will the same success formula still apply? Are the skills the same?

In a word, no. Another client of ours—a large national sales organization—discovered this fact the hard way. Their practice for promoting leaders at the time was decidedly twentieth century. Leaders received promotions and rewards only if they met their sales goals. It did not matter if they "churned and burned" their teams—or worked them so hard that they lost a large portion of their staff to burnout or better opportunities elsewhere. This meant that they were promoting people who could make sales but had virtually no engagement and retention skills. The result? This client suffered from poor customer satisfaction scores. In fact, they were the worst among the top four competitors in their industry. For them, something needed to change, and it needed to change quickly.

But where could they turn? Leadership is a complex subject—so complex, in fact, that if you visit the Barnes & Noble website and search for books on the subject of management and leadership, you will find over fifty thousand titles. The trouble is that the focus of most leadership training largely has been on the skills traditionally associated with leadership, and the values and attributes a leader brings to the job. With this chapter, we present an ambitious premise: It's time to change the mindset of what we look for in a leader. To this point, we have demonstrated that engaged and energized employees that stay and grow with an organization are the key to success. Now we turn our focus to leaders, the people who are the head and the heart of the strategy to engage and retain talent.

The Fish Rots …

In Chapter 5, we discussed how performance was a foundational component of the Career Growth and Accountability Model. The same applies to leadership, although now the significance gets amplified, given the role a leader plays. With our focus on leaders, the thoughtful capability to actively cultivate engagement with one's team members, plus having the knowledge and skills to create workplace conditions that promote retention, become nonnegotiable core competencies for today's leaders. This know-how is essential to every leader's ability to succeed. It is a vital part of team performance, organizational profitability, and long-term success.

The leadership team always—*always*—sets the tone and the culture of the organization. We will get deeper into the culture component in the next chapter. For now, what we need to keep in mind is that, as our colleague Dr. Richard Vosburgh quoted, "A fish rots from the head down." That's an ancient proverb, but it could not be more relevant in twenty-first-century organizational practice. What it means is that the quality of everything we do starts with leaders. In your organization, the "head," your leaders, are the ones who set the tone and culture for their teams. If you don't get your leadership team aligned with the culture you want to promote, then changing that culture and improving engagement is impossible.

Leaders have to fully embrace engagement as a core competency of their jobs. They have to define it in every way possible. This core competency must permeate how leaders carry themselves and conduct their own business with their own teams. Your organization must emphasize engagement skills when promoting leaders into leadership roles and growing them into more and more senior roles.

Leadership sets the tone through their actions and interactions every day. They set the culture for their teams, their partnerships, and their organizations overall. For example, we recently worked on retention with the North American arm of a major European luxury auto manufacturer. On this continent, they have over two hundred car dealerships that are largely run by auto groups that include multiple dealerships and brands under their umbrellas. For those more complex entities, it isn't usually difficult to champion the luxury and exclusivity the brand hopes to promote as part of its mission. However, a significant number of single proprietorships were struggling.

When you charge a premium price for your product, you expect your people to deliver premium service. When that doesn't happen, you have a problem connecting with the customer and keeping them in the fold. So this automaker redoubled its efforts to make exceptional service a part of their culture. When you get a call from one of their technicians or dealerships, the person on the line will ask you, "Is there any reason you wouldn't rate our service as a ten out of ten?" If there is, then the caller will ask if the customer has any advice on how they can correct the problem so they will always rate ten out of ten in the future.

This measure has helped tremendously, but around the time TalentKeepers got involved, the company was still struggling with certain dealerships that weren't living up to the high standard. Upon conducting our surveys, we found that a common characteristic among these dealers was that they were run by a family member—typically a son or daughter of a founding owner—who frankly had no business running a dealership. This often led to disarray from the top down. One center in a southern American city had gone through five general managers in just two years. The general perspective of the senior leadership teams at these kinds of dealerships was, "Well, if that leader's not happy, we'll just get another one." In every instance of these poorer performers, turnover was extremely high, service was rated low, and sales were comparatively poor. The best people at these locations were always quick to flee the environment. This left the dealerships with little choice, they had to rely on people they otherwise probably would not employ.

The Mission Statement

We have already mentioned the old adage that people don't leave companies; they leave bosses. The full picture of why a talented employee leaves for other employment is obviously much more robust than that. For starters, we can add the wisdom of Bruce Belfiore, our colleague from BenchmarkPortal. According to Bruce, the full picture starts with, "Employees don't bond with corporations; they bond with their bosses and colleagues." Sure, a person can believe in a corporate mission, can be proud to work for their company, and can enjoy the benefits of their work, but they don't form their bond with the faceless corporate entity; they form their bond with their boss and coworkers. Either that, or their boss and coworkers break any potential bond before it has a chance to form.

(continued)

The Mission Statement (cont'd)

What this means is that the leader can't only be great at the role her team is responsible for completing. Among many other skills that we will highlight in this chapter, a qualified leader has to buy into and promote the company message. If bonding with the boss is the closest any employee gets to bonding with the company itself, then the boss has to embody the corporate mission. "A good leader needs to know what the corporate mission is," Bruce said, "and especially how it relates to their department and employee interaction. If you leverage this well, you get better results across the board."

Bruce wasn't talking only about retention. He was talking about productivity, efficiency, engagement, and pretty much any other business result a company can track. To illustrate his point, he told us the story of a woman who attended one of his classes five years ago. Bruce was in front of the class, discussing the critical importance of embracing and living the corporate mission as a leader, and he could see this attendee nodding as she rapidly scribbled her notes. "At the end of the class," he said, "she thanked me and told me that the next time I visited her operation, I would see the message in action." During that next visit, the first thing Bruce saw on the wall was the mission statement. It was positioned where it would ensure that it was the first thing that all the agents who worked in this call center would see whenever they walked through the front door for work.

"I see you took the mission statement message to heart," Bruce said, pointing to the sign.

"You were so right about that in the training class," the woman said. "Ever since we started focusing on the mission, we've had better cohesion than I could have imagined. Now we start off every meeting by referring to the mission. It has really brought our teams together."

This might seem like a simple measure at first—and in many ways, it is—but the simplest measures are often the most effective. The corporate mission statement is something that far too many leaders ignore, especially when it's a situation where every leader can find a unifying principle for everything they communicate to their teams. Leaders, and particularly direct report leaders, can and will find this tool especially useful.

Promote for More Than Just Job Skill

Frontline employee turnover is often driven by leadership turnover. We have seen that in every environment in which we have worked. It all starts from the top, no matter what you're talking about. In that last sentence, you can replace the word *turnover* with *engagement,* and it's every bit as true. If you have high leader engagement, you can almost guarantee that you will have high frontline employee engagement. The impact of both realities is easy to see, because it relates to just about every measure of performance you can assess.

If you want high-performing teams that stick together longer and create more meaningful and positive change for your organization, then the leadership team has to embody the message. And just like that call center manager we mentioned in the introduction of this chapter, they have to be *overt* about it. They have to reward leaders who demonstrate not just the ability to get their jobs done at a high level, but the ability to retain and engage their staff. Further, the best organizations have to be willing to part ways with those leaders who don't have that key ability. Keeping the people who deliver the numbers but don't energize their staff is the surest way to underperform over the long term. Driving performance numbers by leaving bruises on your people through fear of negative consequences is not a sustainable strategy. Team members working in these environments will burn out or simply quit after too many verbal beatings.

In an environment committed to energizing employees, we need to select leaders who have a core belief that the best work gets done by inspiring people and lifting them up instead of hammering on them to work ever harder. When looking internally to fill an open leadership role, organizations must interview and evaluate candidates based on how they believe in and support engagement and retention as fundamental requirements of a leader's role. Interviewing internal candidates allows you to base your decision on their track records of energizing employees, too. Do people enjoy working with or for this person? Does this person lift the level of excitement and performance of those people around them? Do people jump at the opportunity to join this person on an assignment, like so many did for Leon?

If you're hoping to hire people from outside your organization, the picture is a little different. You have to *ask* about their record with engagement during the interview process. Make retention a standard criterion that you probe in depth during the interview and selection process. Build in questions that ask the candidates how they inspire engagement, how they build commitment among their employees, what they do to keep people, and how they make their teams more excited about coming in to work.

Fortunately, other tools help assess a candidate's retention skills as well. We will introduce some specific tools in Chapter 8, but later in this chapter, we will discuss how utilizing these assessments can help leaders and prospective leaders identify where their engagement strengths and weaknesses are while also showing them how to improve. Utilizing the assessment allows the organization to develop leaders for the most important skills, thereby building engagement and retention into their leadership development curriculum. An added benefit is improvement in succession planning.

With quantifiable and standardized engagement and retention data at hand, you can compare leader effectiveness and use that data as a key element in identification of potential successors for your best leaders, leaders in key roles, or for areas of your business that need significant improvement. Rather than asking those leaders to engage in the sometimes uncomfortable process of training their eventual replacements, you can identify those potential future leaders through their engagement and retention scores.

Now don't mistake us here. We aren't suggesting that this data should be kept secret. Many organizations make this assessment a secretive process, meaning that a select group of executives get into a room and decide who they're going to target for these positions. But the best organizations are more open about the subject and tell leaders that they need to have someone who's ready to be promoted into their position before they themselves can earn a promotion. Contrary to hurting motivation, this open and honest picture of how to continue on the path up the leadership hierarchy tends to *fuel* a leader's desire to train someone else to take on his role.

When selecting new leaders to serve your organization, the overarching goal is to avoid the common tendency to select or promote someone (whether internally or from another talent pool) based solely on the performance results they're currently delivering rather than a more comprehensive criteria. Include performance results as well as talent engagement and retention results. Many prospective leaders are perfectly capable of delivering business results, but they alienate and demoralize their employees. In other words, these leaders drive performance and deliver short-term results but lose a lot of talent along the way. Organizations often make the mistake of promoting these people based on their results while ignoring the impact they have had on employee turnover. This almost always works out badly for the organization in the short term, but it also can have longer-term impact when these same people continue to deliver great numbers at the expense of their staff and get promoted again and again. The higher the level this kind of leader occupies, the greater the damage they can have on an organization.

Accountability Is Priority 1

"It's not enough to just talk about the importance of engagement," says Steve Urquhart from the Orange County Clerk of Courts in Orlando, Florida. "Nor is it enough to make general statements about our commitment to engagement and retention. Managers have to make it a focus and a part of how they lead. They have to model the behaviors, follow through, and coach the expected performance from their direct reports."

According to Steve, one of the biggest challenges—particularly at the leadership level—is the sense that a leader can manage by decree. In other words, you can make a broad statement about your organization's commitment to a cause and expect everyone to buy in. Some leaders will even write an article in the newsletter and believe that's enough to have everyone modeling the desired outcomes. Whether it's the result of a younger work staff of millennials or a general changing of the times, employees lately are more skeptical about these kinds of measures and are less likely to follow blindly from the bottom up in organizations of all kinds.

For these reasons, none of the measures we have discussed to this point will take your organization where it needs to go without having the leaders *actively* lead the agenda. Leaders can't simply give lip service; employees won't become engaged and will instead keep doing what they've been doing until somebody directly works with them to change. Or worse, employees may become cynical and less engaged with what they perceive as gratuitous support and no action.

"Sometimes senior management overestimates the weight of their proclamations," Steve explained. "Certain messages need to be heard multiple times. Sometimes as an executive, right around the time you're tired of hearing your speech, that's when it starts to sink in."

When it comes specifically to promoting and developing new leaders who are focused on engagement and retention, Steve points out that everybody thinks they want to be promoted, but few people know what's in store for them when they take on a leadership role. "We wanted to provide assessment tools that could provide resources to help that employee engage their readiness and proactively work on some areas that would become a challenge," he said. "Individuals succeed based on their skill set. A manager succeeds based on getting their people to do what needs to be done. That's a tough transition for some people." For this reason, the best organizations take the opportunity to provide some self-development and preparation so prospective leaders aren't walking blindly into a leadership role that might not be a good fit for them. Just as important, the leaders who take charge of these initiatives always hold themselves accountable to provide the necessary training.

You know what's most interesting? Leaders are often surprised to learn that they can make any kind of impact, let alone such a significant one, if they show accountability. "Employees can see and feel senior management's support for them," Bruce Belfiore explained. "And it extends not just through a single team, but across teams and throughout the organization." The trick is that leaders need to take the lead on this matter. They need to make sure their employees feel as if they have a place at the table when it comes to voicing their opinions on matters that they believe will improve their teams, their leadership, and the organization as a whole.

(continued)

Accountability Is Priority 1 (cont'd)

The best practice here is to task your leaders with making sure that proper communication is funneling from one part of your organization to other parts where they can do the most good and be leveraged for the most success. This means leaders getting together to talk about how they can invite people from each other's teams to see other parts of the organization that their daily work does not touch, and meeting people they don't often get a chance to meet. Not only does this instill a better sense of how each employee is a part of the bigger organization, rather than just their own small piece of it, but it also helps leaders and those they lead to see different strategies for energizing and engaging staff as well.

Measuring "Will Do" and "Can Do"

So we know why selecting for engagement and retention competencies is important. We also know that training new leaders on how to lead is key. But how can you shed light on organization-wide data to determine how leaders are performing and how they might learn better engagement strategies from other teams? Many of the employers we work with have found a 360-degree survey format is useful to solicit input from individual leaders themselves, their direct reports, their managers, and often their peers. The objective here is to enhance a leader's awareness of their strengths and weaknesses so that the organization can determine and prioritize the most appropriate developmental activities for that leader. Additionally, this kind of survey can be used as pretraining and posttraining diagnostic tools, and as part of a leadership assessment program for development and promotion.

The content of a survey like this should focus on leadership competencies related to effective employee engagement behavior in both the broad sense, like building trust, as well as being easily customizable to capture organizationally specific content. The results should still retain internal and external benchmarking comparisons that are easy to implement and provide detailed, actionable results to all levels of management, from executive summaries to an individual report for each leader.

Such surveys can make valuable comparisons in those areas where the leader and the other respondents differ in their perceptions. The best way to do this is to keep the survey itself anonymous to ensure that responses are the most transparent possible. When completed, organizations should make the survey available at individual and aggregate levels.

Results often illustrate how a leader perceives him- or herself relative to the perceptions of employees, peers, and managers, guiding the prioritizing of a participant's development plan. As a leader, if you're the agent that promotes this concept, you're seen as a person who is making the team a part of the bigger enterprise. Your team will appreciate you for that, and will see you as someone who not only cares about improving yourself and your employees, but about breaking the team out of the shell and connecting to the organization as a whole.

For senior leaders, the data from this kind of survey can be invaluable, because it enhances your perception of who is and is not ready for promotion either into a leadership role or into a higher level in the organization. This allows you to set up better programs for hiring and training toward better engagement and retention behaviors, and identifying new people for leadership roles. That training is a critical piece of the puzzle as well. "You have to give training that prepares people for their roles as leaders as they advance through the ranks," Bruce Belfiore suggested. "This doesn't often happen. Too often, people are promoted because they're good at what they're doing, but they aren't given training to be a great leader of others."

Another type of assessment is often used to determine promotable readiness for a leadership role. It allows organizations to identify whether their leaders and/or prospective leaders can discern the difference between effective and ineffective leadership behaviors that foster employee commitment and motivation. If the leader or prospective leader can discern that difference, then she will be more likely to succeed in the role. If not, then she probably will not be the best at engaging and retaining talent. This is why measuring where a leader is with her understanding of these principles can take an organization a long way toward ensuring that the best people ascend into leadership roles.

At the same time, many employees who aspire to leadership positions are unaware that they will be dealing with the challenges of engaging employees. This kind of tool helps aspiring leaders fully understand what to expect. Sometimes seeing everything it takes to be a leader will cause less qualified applicants to bow out of the race, which in turn allows organizations to focus only on those people who are best suited for the roles. There are, after all, few things worse than promoting a leader, only to have that leader find that he can't hack it when it comes to motivating, energizing, and keeping talented employees. Often, people ill-fitted for their new managerial roles will switch employers rather than stick around for a demotion. Sometimes these people take great talents with them—talents that would have been extremely valuable to the company if the person hadn't been slotted into a leadership role that didn't suit the employee.

This kind of survey generates results that can be made available for each individual leader and can be aggregated by various attributes. Organizations then use these results to help prioritize the participant's development plan, modify leadership training curricula, and design job aids to help new leaders. This data helps organizations make promotion decisions, but also provides every leader or aspiring leader valuable feedback about what they need to do to get that promotion. Even if an aspiring leader doesn't get the kinds of scores they wanted on this assessment, the message is still, "No worries. Keep working. In fact, here is a list of recommended training programs so you can improve your competency in the areas where you were weak."

Over the ensuing months, those candidates who embrace the need to learn new skills as a prerequisite to being promoted to leadership role speak volumes to their level of interest. Those who do nothing speak just as loudly that they're not going to put any work in and shouldn't be in a leadership role. Those who work hard to improve are willing and able to take that leadership position.

Remember the national sales organization we discussed in the introduction to this chapter? In an environment in which their baby boomer leaders were retiring and the talent pool continued its shift to millennials, they fortunately saw the writing on the wall and made key adjustments to their leadership approach and organizational culture. Since then, they have earned the top spot for customer satisfaction in their industry, literally moving from "worst to first" among their competitors. This is almost entirely because of the significant attention brought to bear on their leaders. They now promote people who are more talented in engagement and retention, they empower them with data from employee surveys, and train them in the full range of leadership skills that engender motivation and create a positive and lively work environment. All of this has led to them keeping more of their best people even in this competitive environment for great talent.

Identification and selection of new leaders is a key process, but the rules in this new era of engagement and retention are different. Broadly speaking, it's not enough to find charismatic and passionate people anymore. You must also look for engagement and retention competencies. The organizations that take the steps necessary will find themselves in the best position to create a culture that inspires engagement and promotes retention.

7 Creating an Engagement and Retention Culture

Think of an organization you know that understands the direct relationship between employee engagement and business success. We work with an employer that commits to town hall–like meetings that formalize company communications and makes them more personal and impactful for leaders and employees at all levels. They hold receptions or dinners where executives speak to a given group about what is happening with the parent organization. At these meetings, the attendees are given the opportunity to ask questions, raise concerns, and make suggestions on how to improve the organization. Now we have a situation in which the groups operating in the field can put names and faces with the people leading the organization and making decisions that impact all employees.

This goal is possible in any organization, and it's only one of many effective components of the engagement strategy Patti McEwen has helped put in place at Sheridan. "All of this has led us to schedule more opportunities for our senior leadership to visit site locations on a regular basis. They used to go once a year, or even never. Now they visit frequently. From the physician side, we've developed our 'Emerging Leaders Program,' which identifies up-and-coming physicians that could be leaders at the local or state level. These potential leaders enter an eighteen-month management training program which has been successful at so many levels that we've recently implemented similar programs for administrative, executive, and nursing staff."

As a result of the corporate buy-in Sheridan pushed for, they're seeing dramatic results from their first survey with TalentKeepers. They have created new and effective initiatives that help employees and leaders all across their remarkably diverse organization, and it has made their culture more cohesive overall. Just as McEwen once saw at DHL, the business results have been clear. Individual sales performance results are always highest with the leaders that score highest on the LEI. "Where I used to see that the best engaged tended to be the longest term and most successful salespeople, I'm seeing that same correlation at Sheridan. The practices with the most engaged leaders are the highest and best performing practices in the organization."

To this point, we've been concentrating pretty much exclusively on how improving engagement and retention works on the individual level. But as Sheridan's story shows, the results ramp up dramatically when you find ways to weave these measures into the organizational culture. In fact, improved engagement and retention always have a positive effect on people and teams, but when organizations embrace these values as part of their culture, the benefits become truly massive.

How massive? In our most recent *Workplace America* survey, when asked, "What part of your company is most impacted by low engagement and high turnover?" respondents placed "morale and culture" in the lead with an eye-opening 65%. The next most frequent response was productivity—seemingly an aspect that most organizations would think about chiefly when discussing workforce turnover—but that trailed culture by a considerable margin, checking in at 63%. Table 7.1 shows the top seven factors impacted by employee disengagement and turnover.

Table 7.1 Top Factors Affected by Employee Disengagement and Turnover

	2018
Morale and culture	65%
Productivity	63%
Team performance	56%
Service quality	53%
Stress	47%
Lost organizational knowledge	45%
Profitability	33%

So here we have plain evidence that the majority of organizations are most concerned about how a lack of energy and commitment to the job can have a negative impact on their culture. The question becomes, how can an organization that understands the value of engagement and retention on employee and leadership levels make those same measures a part of their culture?

As is often the case, finding the answer to this question is a matter of looking to the best-in-class organizations. What are these organizations doing? They start with assessment and analysis. They ask themselves what the organizational climate is like on all levels. They examine how trust and communication might improve. They question whether they are doing enough to stir and embrace creativity and group problem solving. Interestingly, what we have found with these best-in-class organizations is that, after they perform this self-reflection, they report that morale and culture are *not* their top concerns. For the best in class, morale and culture placed third in the *Workplace America* survey, behind productivity and team performance.

How can that be? Are they somehow not placing the importance of culture on the same plane as everyone else? No, it's that the focus on engagement and retention is so true and complete in these cases that the cultural component tends to stitch right in. For best-in-class organizations, the positive energy generated by high engagement and retention are woven into the fabric of the culture. When engagement falls in some areas, only those parts of the organization are affected. Like your body, if you're healthy, even if you suffer the occasional bump or bruise, you still feel good overall. For best-in-class organizations, even with those few leaders or teams that don't focus on engagement and retention as completely as they should, the organization as a whole continues fostering the kind of culture that energizes staff and drastically reduces turnover, and they remain healthy as a result.

Generational Drift

For both best-in-class organizations and those who fall outside that sphere, the chief difficulty expressed in our *Workplace America* research, as well as many other studies, is the challenge to build a high-performing, energized, and positive workplace culture (or culture of any kind) when the workforce is so uncommonly diverse in its wants and needs. The differences between boomers, gen Xers, and millennials is now common in most organizations.

As we have mentioned, millennials officially became the largest generation in the American workplace in 2015. Although they certainly aren't the only ones glued to a smartphone or walking while texting, this tech-savvy talent pool is making waves in every aspect of the workplace, far from the world of start-ups and new-age organizations. This, largely, is good news.

But when it comes to culture building, there is evidence of chafing between the generations at work. Much like the geology of plate tectonics, where continental drift slowly grinds land masses together, this just-below-the-surface pressure may result in trembling or, occasionally, even an earthquake.

To some degree, there always has been and always will be tension between generations. In this year's *Workplace America* study, 80% of all employers asserted that their leaders found challenge in the prospect of managing employees of multiple generations. Further data from our research confirm what many people have expressed about the generational differences. For instance, by and large, millennials seem to be losing patience with the claim that "that's not how we do it around here" whenever they try to put new ideas on the table. Gen Xers and boomers may be wary (or even weary) of the pressure millennials put on the status quo with their heightened expectations and aspirations.

Here's a quote by a study participant, slightly edited so as not to offend our readers. "Dealing with the younger generation is a pain in the [rear]. They want an explanation for all decisions to see if they agree, and if not, they want to argue. Being old school, I sometimes reply with, 'Because I said so, damn it.' But it doesn't help much."

Although this certainly isn't the norm, that sentiment reflects the potential for tension when values, work styles, preferences, and life experiences clash at work. Training will help. The *Workplace America* study shows an encouraging and steady rise in the number of employers that provide formal training on managing multiple generations. Managing millennials is commonly the subject. But many millennials are now assuming leadership roles themselves, which means they are now faced with leading, coaching, and engaging a group of highly tenured boomers.

(*continued*)

Generational Drift (cont'd)

Technology is just one example of a potential area of discord. Virtual meeting tools and e-learning applications will see slight gains in use at work this year. The steady increase in the automation of many human resources processes, for example, performance management platforms, continues to grow. Even as this is happening, some study participants are wondering the best way to deliver company news to younger employees. One avenue is social networks, which are in use by only about 25% of employers today. We expect this to rise in the coming years. As technology continues to evolve and change, and as the workforce gets younger every day, the challenge most organizations face is determining how to stop those tectonic plates from shifting.

Can You Fix Culture?

The cover article of a 2016 issue of the *Harvard Business Review* takes a pretty hard stance on the question we used to title this section. In big orange letters, the periodical says, "You can't fix culture." Obviously, given the existence of this chapter, we take issue with that notion.

They're working from a somewhat common sentiment as well. One participant in the *Workplace America* study said this about where she works, "Anger, fear, and blame dominate our organization's culture." This is a toxic blend of ineffective or wrongheaded leadership beliefs and practices. That's the bad news. The good news is that it's entirely possible to eliminate those toxins. We have seen it again and again at TalentKeepers.

The position taken by the *Harvard Business Review* author promotes the idea that organizational cultures change and evolve as a result of a rigorous and sole focus on executing core business and market strategies. Certainly a dedicated focus on business performance strategies can help get people aligned, see a vision, and understand how they fit into the bigger picture. But too many organizations have bruised and weakened their culture by failing to purposefully cultivate the people held responsible for delivering the business results, day in and day out. Cultures take time and sustained effort to evolve, and the commitment must start with top leadership and work its way down.

The top strategies among best-in-class organizations all revolve around the notion that you have to adapt your culture to *grow*. With the evolution of three generations reshaping the workplace, building your culture will require accommodation and change. Adapting how your workplace operates can reduce friction and enable millennials to contribute their energy and creativity. It's why you hired them. You will need to actively manage and facilitate the process of reinforcing those elements of your culture that contribute to broad success, while introducing new and promising elements that keep your organization moving forward on a successful track.

To build and sustain an energizing and positive culture, engagement and retention must be viewed as a broad organizational and cultural strategy involving all levels of the organization. To combat employee disengagement and unwanted turnover, leaders at all levels must become trust builders. To do this, they must be equipped with the leadership competencies critical for creating committed workforces. Further, if leaders are to own the retention and engagement mission, they must be held accountable and be incentivized for this responsibility.

That said, engagement and retention are not just the domain of the leaders. All employees, including frontline employees, need to be advocates for these missions. They must encourage colleagues to remain with the organization, communicate frustrations to their leaders, and help to build a strong climate of trust and performance.

How do we do that? The approach is multifaceted, and it all springs from that notion we mentioned earlier, about how generational differences and evolving technology create a complicated and moving target. Keeping ahead of demographic trends and generational differences will require new and imaginative ideas, as well as a strong commitment to making retention and engagement a top priority. In short, we must innovate. We cannot expect to continue to use the same methods with an adapting workforce and achieve the same positive results. The future will require creativity and inventiveness to combat the ever-present concerns of turnover and lack of engagement.

Communication Is Still the Key

Now that we have mentioned how important innovation and forward thinking are, let's take a moment to talk about what is arguably the most important strategy—namely, communication. In all matters of organizational strategy, effective communication has to lead the way. If engagement within your organization is like an engine, then effective communication is like the lubricant. Silence is friction. So before we get into the more specific tools and strategies for building an engagement and retention culture, let's discuss that all-important principle that keeps the whole engine running.

According to Bruce Belfiore, most organizations are not very good in the communication department. "Having leaders who excel at communicating with their people is a real sore spot for a lot of companies," he told us. "One thing people don't recognize is that, particularly when they have a multigenerational workforce, they need to tailor that communication so it resonates with the various groups with whom they're trying to communicate."

The focus for an organization attempting to build the right culture is to reshape any communications they receive from executives toward a message that will hook their specific audiences. Different generations perceive messages and respond to them in different ways. "A good leader can think about a communication that needs to be given to each member of the population of employees they have," Belfiore says. "They may reread the communication three or four different times and add different communicative points for each of the target markets so that everyone coming away from that communication will feel the desired connection."

We have found that gen Xers favor community involvement as a way to become more engaged with work. "Generation X likes to have employers who believe in things that they believe in," Belfiore said. "Sponsorship of good causes that they can get involved in goes a long way." It doesn't tend to matter what the cause is, either, as long as it is supporting and advancing something good for the community. The annual run for cancer, bike riding for diabetes, food drives for impoverished youth, and so on—it all serves to help the employee feel more fulfilled in general and bonded to their companies overall. "It isn't just about doing good in the community either," Belfiore told us. "Leaders should also take the opportunity to show employees how their work makes a difference for the company as well."

Whatever the strategy for driving communication and involvement, the top priority should be regular interaction between leaders and employees. Ideally, that interaction should be both personal and professional. Being able to talk to people appropriately about their passions and goals is critical. Belfiore put it best: "The only way you can show someone you care about them as a person is to know them as a person."

Creating the Culture

You know the benefits of building a focus on engagement and retention into your organizational culture. We have also seen how leaders must drive this initiative if it's ever going to work. The question then becomes, how exactly do leaders do that? At TalentKeepers, our experience with these measures has allowed us to identify a range of key strategies. The first step, once someone decides to join your organization, is onboarding.

Onboarding

We describe onboarding as the process that "welcomes a new employee into your culture." The question here is whether you're one of those companies that hires someone, trains them a little, and then throws them into the job, or an organization that strives to make a personal connection from day one and carries that connection throughout the employment life cycle ... and beyond?

A client of ours is a major communications firm, and they face a stiff challenge with new hires, particularly on the retail side of their business. Turnover in retail is often higher than in any other department, so in this situation, they're doing more hiring and training than everywhere else. They used to manage it this way: first the interview, then the hiring, then the employee immediately goes to training, and then once that's complete, they go directly to the store to start working. One of our contacts with this client explained it like this: "What we were seeing was that it was kind of like going to a new high school. If you're the new kid, you feel kind of lost. You have to get your information from a bunch of different sources, and those sources can be confusing at times."

How did this organization overcome? They followed the example of one great frontline leader and made the onboarding process more personal. One manager would reach out to a new hire and meet him at the store before he went to training. In that meeting, he would get the new hire's contact information, introduce him to everyone in the store, and try to connect on a personal level even *before* that new hire was exposed to any form of training. Then, on that first day of training, that great leader would text the new hire, saying something like, "Good luck. You're going to knock it out of the park. We're here if you need anything or have any questions."

That kind of strategy is powerful enough, but this leader also liked to get everyone else on the team involved in the process. Once that new hire got through training, he would have everyone in the store send him an email of congratulations that also welcomed him to the store and offered any help necessary. In this way, the new hire almost always feels more welcome and connected to the organization—and that's all happening before his first real day on the job.

If that seems like a simple measure, that's because it is. And the best part? It's *free*. The cost of an email is just a minute or two of a leader's time. When that communications firm started sharing this as a best practice, they quickly discovered that most markets and almost all levels of the organization saw similar results: new employees were becoming committed and dedicated to the organization quicker and more deeply.

Many organizations have something similar in place for their HR staff to manage, but it is far more important that leaders take an active part of this process. "Handshake" conversations similar to the one our client promotes are an excellent way for leaders and new employees to connect as people and not only as coworkers. Those conversations ideally center on the new employee's career aspirations, leader relationship preferences, engagement and communication, and recognition preferences.

Measuring and Monitoring

One of our discovery exercises when working with organizations interested in increasing retention was to plot all their retention tools on an employee life-cycle timeline. Most of the time, we would see a flurry of activities in an employee's early stages with the organization: recruiting tactics, selection assessments, onboarding processes, initial training tools, and so on. However, most of the time, these tools would diminish or disappear completely after the employee's first sixty to ninety days on the job. We would then plot when new hires were leaving the organization. Not surprisingly, the bulk of the departures came after the retention tactics ended. Creating a culture of engagement and retention is like any other process you are trying to manage; you need frequent measurements to monitor your progress and make adjustments.

Today, 75% of organizations are utilizing some form of survey to measure employee sentiment, whether it's an engagement survey, satisfaction survey, pulse survey, or some other sort of survey. Regularly gathering this data and utilizing the results to measure and monitor how you're doing is essential for sustained execution and success. Following is a partial list of elements this data can help you manage:

1. Measure the effectiveness of each driver of engagement (our research uncovered four engagement drivers illustrated in Figure 2.2) so you can leverage strengths and align resources to opportunities.

2. Monitor progress of initiatives targeting specific engagement elements.

3. Hold leaders accountable for improving opportunity areas.

4. Link engagement metrics to performance measures to build the business case and calculate return on investment.

Action Planning

Once your survey data has been gathered, analyzed, and presented to leadership, the next step is to have concrete, documented action plans based on priorities formed from the results. It's not enough to simply say that you want your leaders and employees to be more focused on engagement and retention. You have to build specific strategies that help weave it into the culture. We have devised a few strategies to maximize the effectiveness of the action planning process. They include the following.

Gifts, Affirmations, and Surprises

Survey results will fall into one of three categories: (1) Gifts are results that are better than leaders expected. Everyone likes gifts, and these can identify strengths that would not otherwise be leveraged. (2) Affirmations are results that are about what leaders expected. They can be strengths or opportunities for improvement, and should be appropriately managed. (3) Surprises are results that are worse than leaders expected. Surprises are often the most valuable, because they can identify "blind spots" leaders would not otherwise identify as opportunities for improvement. As part of the action-planning process, leaders must be prepared for these three types of outcomes, and to expect and value surprises.

Groups, Issues, and People

Action planning should take place at least at two levels: for organizational groups and individual leaders. Senior leaders will want to consider survey results from a group, issues, and people perspective. There will be variance in how different groups performed, and they should be managed differently from an action-planning standpoint. Higher-performing groups can be recognized and studied to see if the practices that led to their higher results may be leveraged as "best practices" and shared with other groups.

Senior leaders should also analyze issues that emerge from the results. Some will be common issues of strength or opportunity across the organization. For these common issues, organizational action plans should be created to identify improvement strategies. Other issues will be unique to certain facets of the organization, and they should be appropriately included in the action plans for these specific areas.

People will also vary in their ability to engage and retain talent. Pay attention to senior leaders and how their teams vary on key engagement metrics. Many times, trends in results within a group can be traced back to the senior leaders who may or may not be aware of the influence they're having through their own behavior and/or messages they're sending down their chains of command. Finally, expect engagement results for individual leaders to vary the most, often using the entire range for the metric. Be sure to recognize those leaders who perform well on both the engagement and performance metrics. Show how their ability to engage and retain talent is facilitating better performance. Support those who perform poorly on both by ensuring that they understand where they have opportunities to improve and ensuring these opportunities are appropriately included in their action plans.

Accountability

As we have been emphasizing from the beginning, the most important goal is to hold your leaders accountable for the engagement and retention of valued and contributing employees on their team.

When I was an executive at Walt Disney Company, a woman we'll call Mindy worked on my team. She was a high-performing professional and a valued member of the group. One day, to my surprise, she came to my office and submitted her resignation to join a small but growing consulting firm in the area. The next day, I walked into my boss's office to share the news, expecting the perfunctory dialogue—the usual, "too bad we lost her; send the requisition form to HR and move on" chat. That's not how it went.

After a thoughtful pause, my boss began with, "What? Mindy quit? How could you let that happen? Why didn't you see this coming? What did you do to try and save her? Who else on your team might be at risk?"

That was just the beginning. Needless to say, I learned an invaluable lesson in leadership that day: *I* was directly accountable for keeping valued team members who might voluntarily resign. I made sure that was the last time I was surprised by a resignation. Every leader in your organization would do well to feel the same way. Engagement and retention only works if the leader holds herself accountable.

Market What You're Doing

Many organizations' wonderful and effective efforts to boost engagement often go unnoticed. Sometimes that's appropriate, but other times, you need to market the engagement actions where you work. Individual recognition goes a long way, but so does recognizing whole teams that meet particularly fantastic goals. Promoting department initiatives is also effective, as is the community involvement we mentioned earlier in the chapter. Whatever the initiative, if you don't promote it a little, it runs the risk of falling flat.

Exit Surveys

At the opposite end of the employee life cycle, exit surveys can be extremely valuable for gathering important data about why people leave. The key point to note here is that exit surveys shouldn't be the *only* kind of survey you ever give to your employees. Later in this chapter and into the next, we'll discuss some specific surveys that have worked extremely well for our clients, but for now, keep in mind that exit surveys are valuable primarily because they sometimes represent the outgoing employee's first real opportunity to feel like she can open up about what went right and what went wrong without having to worry about backlash from a leader or the organization in general. You get the most open and honest answers possible during an exit interview, in other words. Don't let that opportunity go to waste.

You Can't Boil the Ocean

Senior leader support is absolutely essential to the process of building an engagement and retention culture. "What we're finding is that if leaders just give it lip service, people pick up on that and it falls to the wayside," said a client of ours. "So a leader that says and makes a statement that employee engagement is important and backs it up with their actions, we find that's a lot more successful." This might seem obvious, but it's really an important driver of success. You can have everyone from the top down supporting a program, but if the frontline leader is saying, "Engagement is nice, but do whatever you can to make those sales," then the engagement culture isn't going to stick.

A retail client of ours recently had a leader suggest that engagement was his top priority over sales. That kind of statement is a little more dramatic in a sales setting, but the results have been equally dramatic. At a kickoff meeting with all of the organization's frontline managers, that engagement-focused manager shared some of his best practices for how and why engagement was such a critical issue for driving sales and customer satisfaction.

As we mentioned earlier, text messaging is often the simplest and cheapest way to make the kind of connection necessary. That great manager with our retail client told everyone in the kickoff meeting to look at their phones and pick out one employee that reports to them. "Right now, everyone in the room, text that person and tell them thank you for something they've done for you recently," he said, adding an important caveat: "Don't do that for the person who's the top performer that you always recognize. Do it for someone who might be struggling and needs to be recognized." Over two hundred heads in the room looked down at their phones and did exactly that. As the meeting progressed, the surprise and excitement about all the positive feedback these leaders were getting kept building and building.

The central message here is that the connection we're striving for needs to be fostered, and it can't happen only with top performers. If you reach out to people who are struggling, then you build them up and give them the kind of confidence they need to improve. It shouldn't be difficult, because everyone does *something* right. And even with those performers who frequently make mistakes, this strategy opens up the opportunity to coach them on the things that need to be improved. Without that positive connection, coaching only goes so far.

From this lone manager's insight, the company designed a new program that focused on four specific drivers of engagement. The idea was to make every message (1) personal, (2) cool, (3) meaningful, and (4) shaped in a way that improved the employee's chances of success.

"We tell our managers that you can't boil the ocean," our client said. "There's just too much water for you to be able to make that kind of change. But if you focus on these four drivers in everything you do, then you will find success in engaging and retaining more of your people."

The four drivers program has been in place with this client for over a year now, and the data they are picking up has been nothing short of amazing. Engagement and retention measures are at an all-time high. These days, making that personal connection between leadership and frontline employees is a big hallmark of their program, and the results have been tremendous in every measure.

Beyond the organizational philosophies we have covered to this point, other tools can help drive the initiative as well. We will offer more of the specifics about each tool in the appendix, but for now, keep these measures in mind:

The Retention Roadmap

This tool provides a structure with key touchpoints for leaders and other stakeholders in your organization that shows how leadership can connect with new employees at critical points in their early tenure with the organization, such as during week one, upon the completion of new hire training, sixty days in, ninety days in, and so on to build bonds, create comfort, and accelerate productivity.

Assessing for Engagement and Retention Competencies

For new and aspiring leaders, one assessment that we offer is called the Retention Quotient (RQ, for short). RQ is a tool that assesses a leader's knowledge of the elements that drive engagement and retention, as well as their ability to discern what behaviors would lead to higher engagement and retention. It's a "can-do" measurement. If a current or aspiring leader "can" identify better engagement and retention behaviors, then they might "do" right on the job when faced with these decisions. If they can't recognize what "right" looks like, they usually won't exhibit the most effective behavior when presented with the situation.

Using a tool like this to select/promote individual contributors into leadership roles has a dual benefit. By choosing new leaders who recognize effective engagement and retention behaviors, we increase the odds they'll be better stewards of the talent they lead. The second benefit is that we are clearly communicating what it's like to be a leader and the myriad decisions, often in gray areas, they'll have to make. Indeed, some leadership candidates ask, "Are these really the types of situations I'll face in this job?" When affirmed, some will withdraw from consideration, which is far better than being promoted only to learn they are not interested in or suited for the job.

For existing leaders who have been in their roles for three months or more, we offer a survey called Insight. This is a multirater assessment of the ten leadership skills we described in Chapter 2 and have been referencing throughout. The survey provides every leader feedback on how effective they are in applying each of the ten skills from four perspectives: their own self-rating, their manager's, their peers', and their team members'. The results will illustrate areas of strength and opportunity across all rater groups, as well as within and between the raters. Insight is a powerful way to build a leader's awareness and capabilities in engaging and retaining talent.

Of course these tools are only the start. They are only a piece of the puzzle that is creating and sustaining an engagement and retention culture. Surveys are wonderful tools, but what matters most is that your organization does something with the data. The best-in-class organizations will have regular meetings with every leader in the business. In those meetings, they will pore over the readouts of data and use that information to drive best practices for the leader, moving forward. These organizations proactively look for groups and managers who are struggling in specific areas of leadership skills and try to help them. They also follow these strategies regularly, so they can use multiple surveys and years' worth of data to identify trends and use them to find solutions.

Also important is that the best organizations don't look at these meetings as punitive. For those continuously showing low LEI scores or otherwise languishing in the lower categories of engagement, the idea is to use this information as a springboard to help them rather than punish them. This data doesn't reveal shortcomings; it reveals opportunities to coach and train toward greater success. Organizations that do this find that often just one or two factors prevent a leader from becoming great.

No matter how your organization approaches the situation, culture plays a starring role in an employer's success. A vibrant and energized workplace culture does not take root and flourish on its own. Leaders, from the top down, must establish, sustain, and shape high-performance cultures. Above all, these leaders must remember the lessons that trust is the glue that holds a strong culture together, and communication is the lubricant that keeps a high-performing culture growing, supporting creativity, collaborating, competing in a healthy way, and stimulating and promoting individual growth.

8 Building the Business Case for Engagement and Retention

We set out in the beginning of this book to make the case that a motivated, stable, and engaged workforce is essential to the long-term success for your organization—and that an energized workforce is your most important sustainable competitive advantage. It's a business strategy that, to get traction, needs to leverage the strengths of your HR team, enlist operations management, and gain some level of senior management's endorsement. And this means that, in order to sell it and sustain it, you need data to build the case for support, funding to keep the initiatives moving, and mindshare coupled with commitment from those who are required to execute the actions you have planned.

Much of the data you need likely exists. You probably track turnover data already. You may not have attrition information by individual leader, but that is usually obtainable. You should know the cost of losing a valued contributor, as we discussed in Chapter 1. You may also already have in hand many of the relevant key business metrics that are well established and often reported to track performance in your organization.

But this isn't the whole picture. The missing pieces are best obtained through the voice of the employee. In 2018, 73% of companies in the United States administered some form of an employee survey. That's the good news. But there is a glaring problem. A majority of those organizations fail to take meaningful action with the results. Many well-intended employers simply don't have the talent management expertise to turn employee survey data into workable strategies and tactics that can boost business results and contribute to long-term success. In most cases, the problem is that those in the know are not properly demonstrating the metrics that matter to organizational success. This is where it all begins—with the knowledge of the metrics that matter.

Examples of Metrics That Matter

66% of all 887 organizations that participated in the most recent *Workplace America* study were able to raise customer satisfaction as a result of their engagement and retention initiatives.

Links between customer satisfaction and increased sales are well established.

100% of this year's best-in-class organizations track links between on-the-job safety and employee engagement and satisfaction.

55% of all United States organizations link engagement to performance. Those that do make this link see a tremendous competitive advantage.

The real value in linking key performance indicators like these to employee engagement, and determining where the largest gains are, is to determine where best to invest limited resources to get the biggest payoff. See Figure 8.1 for the top performance metrics impacted by higher engagement and retention.

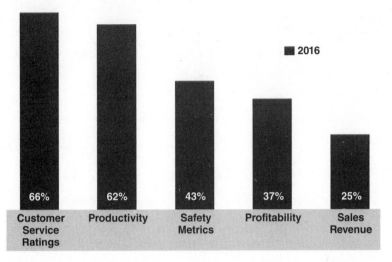

Figure 8.1   The top performance metrics impacted by higher engagement and retention.

Where's the Money?

For as long as we have been working in this sphere, it has always shocked us how resources, particularly in light of the known impact an engaged and stable workforce can have on performance and profitability, are so hard to build into established budgets. Across the American workplace, employee engagement budgets have fallen for four straight years. In 2014, 71% of all employers carved out some level of funding for employee engagement. By 2018, it was down to 54%. Are executives and finance chiefs saying that customer service, safety, sales, culture, and profitability are less important than they used to be?

The best-in-class organizations all dedicate some of the highest percentages of their labor and operations budgets to engagement strategies. One approach we have long advocated is to move a number of essential employee initiatives (e.g., onboarding, wellness programs, benefits, incentives, training, leadership development) under an "Engagement" budget category for the sole purpose of bringing attention to the importance of this key aspect of talent management.

Finding the Money

Over the course of this book, we have provided the data, insights, and tactics that will help you turn these bigger ideas into action. As we make our final kick to the finish line, we provide a series of strategies that will help you fund your engagement and retention initiatives and help ensure the greatest level of success. We begin with the funding:

1. **Work from data and build your case.**

   Here, you will want to focus on relevant and accepted metrics that link engagement/retention to business results. It also helps to gather new metrics wherever helpful. Be sure to use current sources of data such as retention statistics.

2. **Establish or build budget categories for engagement and retention.**

   We advise this approach because you may find that one strategy will be easier to fund than another. Be thoughtful about where this budget resides in your business unit and who controls the funds (HR? Operations? Training?).

   Next, move existing funded activities into this bucket to create the understanding that you are already doing some things that contribute to keeping and motivating people. Include everything we have covered in this book, such as onboarding activities, employee communications channels, employee-appreciation activities, volunteer and community service programs, fitness facilities, employee surveys, service awards, and so on. The purpose of this step is to establish the mindset that this initiative is important.

3. **Recruit and foster internal partners and advocates.**

   As with any major initiative, recruiting thought leaders in various parts of the business to serve as your advocates and supporters is the first step. Find leaders who believe in your mission, have influence, and will support you in getting resources and funding.

Their ability to help you gain that funding is invaluable, but they can also help you during the execution phase as well.

Spreading the Impact

Next, let's look at how you can lay the groundwork for the most successful engagement and retention initiative possible.

1. Start where you will succeed.

With so many moving parts and people contributing opinions, start your new initiative or tactic with a manageable business unit that has a strong and supportive leader who has demonstrated an ability to embrace and execute a new program or process. It's always tempting to start with the worst retention department in your organization, but don't be lured into this common trap. Your goal should be to start where you have the highest probability of success, where you can demonstrate positive results. Then later, after you have launched and implemented the process with the friendlier group, you can go after the more challenging ones.

2. Brand it and promote it.

Branding an initiative gives it what marketers like to describe as "legs." That means it has the potential to expand and grow into new areas. You likely do this now with other major projects or launches. It's a well-known way to use a single phrase, term, or label to communicate the breadth, depth, values, and goals of the effort.

3. Stick to it and sustain execution.

It goes without saying that nothing ever reaches a positive conclusion without follow-through. In this case, the message is to hold people accountable for whatever you ask them to do. Check in regularly. Schedule regular, brief chats with key people. Track and report activities. Like any important effort, it takes time for these strategies to take hold and demonstrate their impact. The name of the game is to keep it going!

4. Leverage results and set the hooks.

Make engagement and retention a standing topic in management meetings. Use these meetings to change how you discuss turnover. Percentages are fine for high-level tracking and comparison purposes, but for the most impact, personalize the turnover by talking about a specific person (exit data you may have, where they are going, and so on). Have the leader of that person do the talking, and ask that leader probing questions like, "Did you see it coming?" "Is anyone else in your department at risk?" and so on.

The bigger goal here is to find ways to weave the vision and beliefs into your culture. As we mentioned earlier, start small. The old adage "Success breeds success" is as true today as it has ever been. Remember the national telecommunications client of ours that went from worst to first on the J. D. Power survey of customer satisfaction? They attribute that success to a focus and determination to improve the customer experience by retaining frontline employees and training leaders on how to engage and inspire them.

Connecting Engagement with Success in Telecom

According to Jim Bowles, "We believed in the notion that people didn't leave companies, they leave their managers." Jim discovered this underlying wisdom during his time as vice president of workforce development at AT&T. With this wisdom, we come full circle to that old nugget that people don't quit organizations, they quit bad bosses. Viewed from a reverse angle, "That interface between employee and their direct supervisor is the most critical element for the success of the organization."

When Bowles and AT&T set out to find tools that could improve employee engagement and the likelihood of retention, they turned to TalentKeepers' strategies because they made sense and were easy for managers to grasp and apply. "That's such a key element of this because you can get caught up in so much theory," Bowles explained. "And managers aren't as interested in that. They want to see results and want to see that this is helping them be successful."

So the simplicity is key. "Managers want to move on," Bowles said. "They're pressured to be successful and deliver results. They're confronted with 30,000 leadership books and various approaches on how to be effective leaders. But what they really need is to build and strengthen their relationships with the people who work with them. If they do that, then all their other needs as managers will be met."

So according to Bowles, what were the key factors to getting the initiative funded and achieving success? "The buy-in had to be supported from top to bottom. We had to set up reinforcement mechanisms tied to performance management systems. Everybody wants to have the magic bullet, but engagement and retention is never about one size fits all. It's about beating the drum on the fact that you have to treat employees individually and focus on their uniqueness. Doing this increases the likelihood of success significantly.

"Of course there has to be a return on investment for the organization, so a key element of success for us was to tie engagement metrics to sales and service performance. The correlation was clear, and this not only provided a strong ROI for the organization, but a real 'what's in it for me' or 'WIIFM' for every leader involved."

Building a Winning Strategy

Finally, let's take one last step back to reexamine what a winning strategy looks like:

1. Leadership accountability

Leaders are a relatively low-cost asset (you already pay them) in the battle to engage and retain the quality of talent you need to succeed, compete, and grow. The importance of holding them accountable for this part of their roles cannot be overstated. It's what you promoted them to do. Every leader should have engagement and retention goals, incentives to meet those goals, and consequences for failing to do so.

2. Adapt your culture to grow

With the evolution of three generations reshaping the workplace, building your culture will require accommodation and change. Adapting how your workplace operates can reduce friction and enable millennials to contribute their energy and creativity. It's why you hired them. You will need to actively manage and facilitate the process of reinforcing those elements of your culture that contribute to broad success, while at the same time introducing new and promising elements that keep your organization moving forward on a successful track.

3. Career growth and stay interviews

Many dynamics are at work that can prompt good workers to stay or leave. And one thing is certain: a positive, constructive relationship between each leader and his or her direct reports, based on trust and communication, provides your best shot at inspiring commitment and engagement in your employees. Require leaders to hold periodic stay interviews with each employee. Opening that dialogue is your first swing at combating job and career issues and keeping good people longer.

4. Watch the metrics

Employee engagement surveys once again remain the most common engagement tactic for a good reason: You need data that provides a roadmap on where to apply energy and resources to strengthen your organization. Metrics are ubiquitous today. Use them to your advantage to build on existing strategies or to launch and execute new ones. Track and report results. Educate your organization on the importance of an energized workforce.

5. Be aggressive and drive execution

Keep pushing. Be the champion of an engaged workforce. Expect your organization to be a place where everyone is proud to work and success is assumed. Reward good leaders. Replace or reassign poor ones. This comment from the most recent *Workplace America* study may say it best: "Employee engagement and retention is currently very good at my organization, but we continue to work on new initiatives to improve and strengthen our employee culture each year."

TalentKeepers is proud to be a leader in shaping how people view engagement and retention in the workplace, and to develop innovative solutions to help organizations everywhere engage and retain employees. Our hope is that this book has helped you identify those strategies best suited for your culture, needs, and budget.

APPENDIX
TALENTKEEPERS ENGAGEMENT
AND RETENTION SOLUTIONS

TalentKeepers' Experience and Capabilities

TalentKeepers® was founded in 2000 to conduct global research on why highly valued employees choose to join, stay, and leave organizations. Our findings have enabled us to develop proven solutions for the most challenging talent management issues. Partnering with organizations in virtually every industry around the world, we continue to find that optimizing employee engagement is one of the greatest unmet opportunities in business today. The criticality of employee engagement is not subject to the vagaries of the economy; employers always need to engage their talented people, whether during times of little or rapid growth. Securing the future of the organization resides in your people.

TalentKeepers is well experienced in the human resources industry, specializing in talent management, with award-winning solutions in onboarding, employee engagement, leadership development, employee retention, and other key talent management areas. Our team of industrial/organizational psychologists will work collaboratively with you to develop a talent management strategy, correlate results to your key business metrics, and execute strategies that get results.

How will we accomplish this? We'll work with you in attacking organization, job and career, coworker, and leader factors that keep high performers engaged. We also provide ongoing analytic information that enables you to monitor and benchmark the impact of the four factors that influence peoples' decisions to join, stay, or leave. Predictive information will allow you and your organization to take proactive and preemptive action. With our solutions you can build a culture that keeps your best talent, boosts productivity, and cuts labor costs.

In addition to partnering with organizations, since 2004, TalentKeepers has conducted *Workplace America*, the longest continuously running study on employee engagement in the United States. This research allows us to better understand the cost, causes, and consequences of disengaged employees and to share proven strategies that help keep your employees top of mind and engaged.

Our Mission

Our mission is to build insight, knowledge, and understanding for individuals and organizations about the world of work around them and provide solutions to increase commitment, engagement, and desire to excel.

Our Core Values

Adapt to unlock potential

Teamwork and collaboration

Assume positive intent

Responsiveness

Growth through innovation

Provide service with a personal touch

Commit, Engage, Excel

TalentKeepers' Engagement Continuum: Commit

Getting employees to connect and commit to the organization is imperative for building engaged, loyal, and productive team members. Organizations that are successful in achieving this enjoy the following benefits:

Strengthened bonds with the new leader and team

Commitment to organization, leader, and role

Increased speed time-to-productivity

Accelerated acclimation and assimilation

Reduced early turnover

Facilitated alignment with goals and objectives

Step one of this process sometimes means going back to the basics. Developing recruiters and hiring the right talent is critical for organizational success. By supporting the recruiting process, your organization will:

Provide tools to reduce early tenure attrition.

Include recruiters and other key stakeholders (e.g. trainers) on processes that guide key interactions with new team members within the first ninety days of employment.

Hold recruiters and other key stakeholders accountable for new hire retention goals.

TalentKeepers' Engagement Continuum: Engage

Engaged employees provide "discretionary effort" every day to help their organization achieve success. When organizations are able to create and maintain an engaged workforce, they enjoy an organizational culture that

Sustains high engagement among all levels

Enables individual performance

Empowers leaders through awareness and coaching

Builds team performance

Measurably impacts customer experience (+ NPS, + ENPS)

Significantly improves retention

TalentKeepers' Engagement Continuum: Excel

Helping your employees adapt to new challenges and needs as well as excel in their roles is an ongoing challenge. Your organization is invested in these employees and motivated to coach and develop them to their fullest potential. Organizations that know how to create this atmosphere enjoy the following outcomes:

Effectively manage change at all levels

Leverage experience to energize the culture

Foster career growth regardless of the trajectory

Enable leaders to focus on and prioritize development areas

Avoid "quit and stay" and other plateauing behaviors

Guide HIPOs through transitions

Facilitate cross-functional collaboration

ABOUT THE AUTHORS

Christopher Mulligan, Chief Executive Officer, TalentKeepers

Chris has over 30 years of experience in the human resources industry, the majority of which has been in the employee engagement, selection, assessment, and retention arena. Chris co-founded TalentKeepers in 2000, an organization dedicated to the issue of employee engagement and retention. *Human Resource Executive* Magazine has twice recognized TalentKeepers products as "Top Training Products of the Year." Chris has worked with organizations around the world on employee engagement and retention issues including: Accenture, AT&T, BMW, Coke, GE, Marriott, and UPS.

Chris is a national speaker on employee engagement and retention. He has coached senior leadership teams and written numerous chapters, articles, and research reports on how to improve performance through people. Prior to co-founding TalentKeepers, Chris was the vice president of business development for AlignMark, a division of Thomson Reuters.

Chris is a member of the American Psychological Society and an Associate Member of the Society for Industrial and Organizational Psychology. He holds a BS in psychology from the Florida State University and an MS in industrial/organizational psychology from the University of Central Florida.

Craig R. Taylor, former Vice President, Client Services, TalentKeepers

Craig R. Taylor is the former vice president of client services at TalentKeepers, where he led the client services team responsible for all client engagements. He joined TalentKeepers in 2002. In 2018 he retired from full-time work to dedicate his time to writing, speaking, and sailing.

Craig has been a well-known leader in the corporate training, organizational development, and performance improvement profession for over 25 years. He spent many years as an executive with The Walt Disney Company as director of the Disney Institute. Earlier in his career, Craig spent several years at American Express Company managing leadership assessment and evaluation, leadership training, and career development strategies. Craig also worked at Wilson Learning Corporation, a global training and consulting firm where he led the corporate consulting practice. He has been an adjunct professor of psychology at several colleges and universities.

Craig is an award-wining author and frequent speaker at national conferences and events. He has chaired the editorial advisory board and served on the "e-Learning Brain Trust" for the top training and development industry publication *TD Magazine*, where he has served as a contributing editor and regular columnist. He has authored numerous feature articles on leadership, employee engagement and talent management, and is a past winner of the Walker Award for Article of the Year in *People and Strategy Journal*.

Craig received his undergraduate degree in psychology and an MEd and EdS in counselor education, all from the University of Florida.

INDEX